Keener Sounds

Selected Poems from
The Georgia Review

Edited by

STANLEY W. LINDBERG

and

STEPHEN COREY

THE UNIVERSITY OF GEORGIA PRESS
ATHENS AND LONDON

© 1987 by the University of Georgia.
Because this page cannot legibly accommodate the
copyright credits for individual poems reprinted
here, pages 223 and 224 of this book serve as an
extension on this copyright notice.
Published by the University of Georgia Press
All rights reserved
Designed by Ronald F. Arnholm
Set in Janson typeface with Caslon display headings and printed
by letterpress on 50 pound Warren's Olde Style at Heritage Printers,
Inc., Charlotte, North Carolina

The paper in this book meets the guidelines for permanence and durability
of the Committee on Production Guidelines for Book
Longevity of the Council on Library Resources.

Printed in the United States of America

91 90 89 88 87   5 4 3 2 1

Library of Congress Cataloging in Publication Data

Keener sounds.

1. American poetry—20th century. I. Lindberg,
Stanley W. II. Corey, Stephen, 1948–   .
III. Georgia review.
PS613.K4   1987   811′.54′08   86–25086
        ISBN 0–8203–0936–2 (alk. paper)
        ISBN 0–8203–0937–0 (pbk.: alk. paper)

British Library Cataloging in Publication Data available.

Keener Sounds

This book is dedicated by the current editors of
The Georgia Review

to the memory of

JOHN DONALD WADE (1892–1963)
Founder & Editor, 1947–50
JOHN OLIN EIDSON (1908–1983)
Editor, 1950–57
WILLIAM WALLACE DAVIDSON (1901–1978)
Editor, 1957–68

and to the honor of

BETTY L. SARGENT
Business Manager, 1965–77
Assistant Editor, 1977–82
JAMES B. COLVERT
Editor, 1968–72
WARREN LEAMON
Assistant Editor, 1968–71
EDWARD KRICKEL
Assistant Editor, 1971–72
Editor, 1972–74
STEPHEN MALONEY
Assistant Editor, 1972–74
JOHN T. IRWIN
Editor, 1974–77

Contents

[ix]

[x]

Introduction

Just as in *Necessary Fictions* (1986) we attempted to gather the most memorable stories published during *The Georgia Review*'s first forty years, in this book we present what for us are the most compelling poems featured since our 1947 founding. Much of the vitality informing American poetry in recent decades is captured, we believe, by the inviting diversity in this gathering of 143 works by 120 different voices: poems—narrative, lyric, and dramatic—in a variety of traditional and open forms, ranging in length from a dozen lines to five hundred. Yet each individual piece serves to remind us as well of important continuities in poetry through the centuries. Each exhibits, in its own way, what Wallace Stevens has called "The maker's rage to order words"—words that speak tellingly

> ... of ourselves and of our origins,
> In ghostlier demarcations, keener sounds.

The *keener sounds* in Stevens' poem (and in the title of this anthology) are, of course, much more than just the auditory effects of the words themselves. Stevens is referring to—and illustrating—the more complex sounds of poetry, the potential richness and layering of language that humans strive for in giving expression to their most discerning and intense perceptions of the world.

The editorial problems we faced in making these selections were even more difficult than those we had encountered earlier with the fiction anthology. *The Georgia Review* has published more than 1,300 poems (over half of these within the past ten years), and the spectrum of voices and styles is significantly greater than in the stories—in part because the various editors of *The Review* differed more in taste and in part because there have been, since World War II, more dramatic and wide-reaching shifts in American poetry than in fiction. In a very few cases (most notably those of Conrad Aiken, Robert Graves, and Byron Herbert Reece), our choices were influenced by such historical factors as the proclaimed regional focus of the journal in its early years and the general critical consensus regarding twentieth-century poets. Our primary concern, however, was to find those poems that continue to speak most clearly and deeply, regardless of their makers' fame or lack thereof, and we are delighted that the final grouping contains not only many poets with established reputations but also a number of lesser-known yet highly accomplished writers. Several of the poets—Kathryn Stripling Byer, Alice Golembiewski Phillips, Pamela Kircher, Scott Minar, and Marilyn Nelson Waniek—achieved their first national publication in *The Georgia Review* and are now earning larger audiences through subsequent work.

Inevitably, many fine poems and poets must be excluded from any retrospective gathering, and none of the poets selected could be featured in depth. We wish these circumstances could be otherwise, of course, and we urge readers to supplement our choices by going directly to the poets' books, many of which are still in print. Good libraries have most of them; good readers should, too.

Because poets tend to pay such close attention to their poetic ancestors and to memory in general, they are frequently accounting for what is lost as well as what remains—that is, they are often concerned, at some level, with elegy. The poems of *Keener Sounds* offer many subjects, tones, and moods, but their most common touchstone is loss: of home, of innocence or faith, of some friend or family member. A few of the poems are laments for poets who have died in recent years, and we turn now briefly to this special group because they are particularly powerful reminders of the importance of continuity, and community as well, among artists.

Poets seem drawn to eulogize their own. Because the words of the dead still live, the passing of the body and mind creates a special poignance, one born of both fear and faith. Through elegy, the living poet comes to touch the reality of loss which the deceased poet's writing has worked so hard to deny; but then, the one who remains will often turn again, absorbing the fact of death by going back to what stays—the poems.

At the midpoint of "This Day After Yesterday," Philip Booth's remembrance of Robert Lowell, the speaker comes to this impasse: "Weighed by your dying, / Cal, I find myself / much wanting." Then Booth tries to tell himself he is somehow better off with Lowell gone, but the ploy does not work: "Everything about me / sags: my body tells / my disbelief its / own mortal story." Solace comes only when Booth steadies his eye on Lowell's work, the poems that can generate toward their author—in this world and the next—the same love that old Argos showed upon the homecoming of Odysseus: "*May all such ghosts attend / your spirit now. May it, / with them, be lighter.*"

Richard Hugo, in "Last Words to James Wright," goes through a similar refusal and acceptance—guided to the latter, again, by the deceased poet's work. Hugo recalls a private joke he shared with Wright (each called the other "Ed Bedford") and Wright's assurance that his cancer surgery would be successful: "I took that as a promise. I really did. / Ed Bedford, you bastard, you lied." Although Hugo feels in his poet-friend's passing a crucial weakening of his own life—"the starker the fact I'm facing / the less I want to sing"—his tribute, like Booth's, rides an upward curve at its ending. "Be glad of the green wall you climbed across one day. / Be glad as me," Hugo implores, reaching back to Wright's first book (*The Green Wall*) for an image of the effort involved in the poet's whole career.

Many other poets have written elegies for Lowell and Wright. Hugo's early death in 1982 followed Wright's by only two years, and a great number of poems for Hugo already have appeared. Clearly, despite occasional private or public feuds, most poets know and care about one another (and one another's work) in vital ways. Indeed, their community of like-tending spirits—present in one form or another since the time of Homer and probably beyond—seems to have become increasingly important as the global village has evolved to link and yet isolate nearly everyone in the contemporary complex of products, money, and power.

Lately there has been some criticism aimed at the so-called "bureaucracy" and "mafia" of contemporary poetry, terms accusingly proposed because more and more poets have come to be associated with universities, writers' conferences, and other institutionalized poetry centers. The prospects for cronyism and for homogenized thoughts and styles are certainly real whenever poets come together in such formalized circumstances; but we believe that *Keener Sounds*—many of whose authors are connected with institutions in one way or another—offers strong evidence that the pulse and yawp of American poetry have scarcely been stifled. Poets always have done whatever they could to reach and learn from their masters and peers. In previous centuries, distance and circumstances often limited poets to reading the works of others and, in some cases, corresponding by mail. In our own time, however, the technologies of communication and transportation have allowed poets to reach one another more often and in more ways: public poetry readings have become frequent since the days when only a few—Robert Frost, Carl Sandburg, Vachel Lindsay—went out on the road; phonograph records, cassette tapes, and even video tapes of poets reading and talking are now widely available. Support for this growing poetry community has come from various sources, but the colleges and universities across the country have been by far the most consistent and generous in their efforts: they fund readings, they give employment to writers, and they provide a way for developing writers to make contact with authors of known talent and accomplishment.

Thus, the past or present academic positions held by some of the poets featured here should come as no surprise, and neither should the fact that others here have come along on different routes. Greg Kuzma is a professor of English in Lincoln, Nebraska, while Ted Kooser is a businessman in the same city; neither poet was better or worse equipped, by virtue of his employment alone, to write the fine poems reprinted in this anthology. All serious poets are members of a small but vital community who understand that the "rage to order words" has always been an impulse shared with others—however few, however scattered. Poets must create themselves on their own, but often they can improve themselves by learning from the writing community.

Such learning, professional and personal, takes place in our time both because of and in spite of the many contacts among poets. Charles Edward Eaton studied with Robert Frost. W. S. Merwin traveled to Majorca to apprentice under Robert Graves. Cathy Smith-Bowers learned from Susan Ludvigson, Bin Ramke from Stanley Plumly and Wayne Dodd. Anne Sexton and Maxine Kumin were neighbors, and Alice Golembiewski Phillips was a student of Kumin. Philip Levine studied with John Berryman, Robert Penn Warren with John Crowe Ransom. Such a listing could go on and on, delineating hundreds of additional academic and personal conjunctions—and all this without beginning to suggest the enormous continuing influences exerted by such earlier makers as Shakespeare, Keats, Dickinson, Whitman, and Rilke.

The "years" of the poems that follow encompass four decades so far as their publication dates are concerned, but there is an important sense in which this volume stretches back more than one hundred years to the birth of Frost and Aiken, shortly after the Civil War. In the year of Frost's birth, it is worth noting, both Whitman and Dickinson were still vigorously productive. The line of American poetry seems not so long after all, if seen in this way—the way that the poets so often see, the way of the unbroken circle.

With this collection we salute all members of this circle, especially those poets who have enriched our pages over the years. We view this retrospective both as an honoring of *The Georgia Review*'s fortieth year and as a celebration of poetry, the apparently fragile yet persistent art that strives to make language fresh and unique—ever keener—in a culture which too seldom rewards or even recognizes such crucial effort.

SWL & SC
Athens, Georgia

Dannie Abse

Bedtime Story

Adam, the first man, my father said, perfect
like the letter *A*. Blessed be all alephs.
Then my clever question: were there no creatures,

father, before Adam? A long index finger
vertical as a flame to horizontal lips.
Eyes right, eyes left. Whisper of a spy:

yes, unfortunate creatures, angels botched,
badly made, born to be vagrant, born with
the usual amnesia but with little sense

and no sense of direction. They could not
deliver the simplest of messages . . .
Now, late, I think of that flawed lineage:

of one announcing great news to the wrong Mary
—perhaps it was that unshaved derelict
at the bus station with an empty bottle, muttering—

and here's another in disguise, down at heel,
defeated face white as the salt of Sodom,
veteran among the homeward football crowd

shuffling under hoardings towards nightfall;
and this one supine, overbearded,
sleeping on a park bench in his excrement.

Dogs bark and bark at them.   They lack pleasure.
They refrigerate the coldness of things.
They stale. They taste the age of their own mouths.

In Casualty rarely cry or grumble.
In wards die with only screens around them.
But now, father, here's *my* bedtime story:

sometimes in the last light of January,
in treeless districts of cities, in a withered
back street, their leader can be glimpsed from trains.

He stands motionless in long black overcoat
on spoilt snow and seems like a man again
who yet, father, will outlast the letter Z.

A Winter Visit

Now she's ninety I walk through the local park
where, too cold, the usual peacocks do not screech
and neighboring lights come on before it's dark.

Dare I affirm to her, so agèd and so frail,
that from one pale dot of peacock's sperm
spring forth all the colors of a peacock's tail?

I do. But she like the sibyl says, "I would die";
then complains, "This winter I'm half dead, son."
And because it's true I want to cry.

Yet must not (although only Nothing keeps)
for I inhabit a white coat not a black
even here—and am not qualified to weep.

So I speak of small approximate things,
of how I saw, in the park, four flamingoes
standing, one-legged on ice, heads beneath wings.

Betty Adcock

Nothing Happened

That year the doves sounded autumn early,
the town a knot among the fields
that hummed a sound like a schoolroom.
Blackberries put on their last slow dark
near our house. The sun would set
a tin roof blazing and a lame man cut
tall grasses with a scythe.
Days fell like yellow snow on every farm
though weeks at a time
nothing was the same.
Once or twice words jutted from a page
and some photographs leaked the future
like the foreign light a blow lets in your eyes.
Those moments my ribs would leap
and something settled would shape itself,
a thin metallic winter unlike
winter, unlike anything,
would come under the breastbone.
Of course it did not really come.
Not then.

There were people whose skin I remember
the smell of. They came that close.

Conrad Aiken

The Walk

Profound, profound and brief
this talk of joy and grief
from night of womb
to night of tomb—

how short a walk we have
before we find a grave,
just learn to stand, and then
fall down again—

a few words learn to say,
to pray or not to pray,
or tune a simple song,
but often wrong—

try learning of love, too,
confused by "I" and "You,"
and O what trouble make
of that dear give-and-take—

so seldom look above
the dark self-love,
see almost nothing
beyond self-loathing!

Time, give us time to know
whether to stay or go,
to make the choice also
of yes and no,

that looking backward we
our forward selves may see,
thus each way free
the ought-to-be.

[4]

Heather Allen

The Cartographers

Haunted by an offshore wind,
A radiance just out of reach, the horizon
Like the threshold of an open door,
The known cannot hold them.

In the field they hear
The swiftly beating hearts of birds,
And feel the deer's dark eye—

Watch the wind's path
Sink in the tall grass,
And the thread the birds unwind
At the limit of sight.

In a circle of trees
Facing outward, bodies linked
More closely to defend
The secret clearing,

There is a maze where light and leaves
Have equal body, and the birds
Disappear into bowers of air,
Sharp and swift as yearning.

To see how solid things are shadowed
By a luminous transparency
Is to discover
How this world maps another—

It is for their art to show
The shape the birds design, their spiral flight
The subtle circling of fate,
The twists of time;

To draw the bodiless and shifting trees
That live in a quiet pool,
And render its deceptive clarity, its light
The light of memory—

Where scenes of deepening brilliance rest
Like the bright stones on the bottom,
Out of reach.

Just how far away
That brightness is
No map can show—
Its art can bring us only to the edge

Of the secret center
In the labyrinth of trees,
The paths that die out
In the forest, mountains, sea—

The unyielding distance
Cartographers call
Strange beauty.

John Ashbery

Märchenbilder

Es war einmal . . . No, it's too heavy
To be said. Besides, you aren't paying attention any more.
How shall I put it?
"The rain thundered on the uneven red flagstones.

The steadfast tin soldier gazed beyond the drops
Thinking of the hat-shaped paper boat, that soon . . ."
That's not it either.
Think of the long summer evenings of the past, of the
                                        Queen Anne's lace.

Sometimes a musical phrase would perfectly sum up
The mood of a moment. One of those lovelorn sonatas
For wind instruments was riding past on a solemn white horse.
Everybody wondered who the new arrival was.

Pomp of flowers, decorations
Junked next day. Now look out of the window.
The sky is clear and bland. The wrong kind of day
For business or games, or for betting on a sure thing.

The trees weep drops
Into the water at night. Slowly couples gather.
She looks into his eyes. "It would not be good
To be left alone." He: "I'll stay

As long as the night allows." This was one of those night rainbows
In negative color. As we advance, it retreats; we see
We are now far into a cave, must be. Yet there seem to be
Trees all around, and a wind lifts their leaves, slightly.

I want to go back, out of the bad stories,
But there's always the possibility that the next one . . .
No, it's another almond tree, or a ring-swallowing frog . . .

[7]

Yet they are beautiful as we people them

With ourselves. They are empty as cupboards.
To spend whole days drenched in them, waiting for the next whisper,
For the word in the next room. This is how the princes must have
                                                              behaved,
Lying down in the frugality of sleep.

Whether It Exists

All through the fifties and sixties the land tilted
Toward the bowl of life. Now life
Has moved in that direction. We taste the conviction
Minus the rind, the pulp and the seeds. It
Goes down smoothly.

At a later date I added color
And the field became a shed in ways I no longer remember.
Familiarly, but without tenderness, the sunset pours its
Dance music on the (again) slanting barrens.
The problems we were speaking of move up toward them.

Coleman Barks

The Last Rebirth

To fix attention on the dead
and not let us wander off
a clamp shuts in the chest.
Lights grow faint and more numerous.
There's only the looking in.

Your palm
beneath the outer map of skin
has an old wound badly sewn up
with ordinary white thread
healed in an ugly welt
that opens while you look.

Inside the hand, a host
the small image of a man
wrapped in membrane like a toy
that's been buried in the earth.
You've been tending him for years
within your body
loving the bare backs of women
placing your right hand in cold streams
for him, and now you know why.

What world you've known, the sky itself
is densely rooted and nerved
here in this icon
your one true pregnancy
still on the bloodvine like a melon
perfecting its stripes
with seeds and memory.

The dead are way ahead of us, thank God,
at the clean wooden tables by the waterfall
in the permanent mist

talking however they do
without using metaphor.
Left behind we meditate on something,
on a pair of pliers
changing the bite, open and shut.

Wind ruffles a quilt
slowly through a week of weather.
A crowd with all ages dancing, hands in the air
come to the presence of trees where each
inside himself rejoices
like fish in shallow rapids
or any other sign
say the edge of a door
or a man running down a flight of steps
signs the last rebirth
hasn't yet begun.

Gerald W. Barrax

The Competitors

We still call it mother
and taken without love or care
she bears the weight of our faults,
in her huge orgasms grinding her teeth along her own faults
and shaking our buildings down.
If we counted her bodies and our own
we'd see how little help she needs.
But we do help
with engines invented by cunning men
    catapult, ballista, springal, trebuchet
    throwing swarms of arrows spears stones
    crossbows and Greek fire
to do to flesh what they will.
    At that she sighs in another ecstasy
and turns her winds to widow's work
blowing our buildings down,
knowing we have our own ways to help her
with devilish devices invented by disinterested men
    gunpowder, cannon, mortar, rocket
    aircraft, bomb
to do to flesh what they will.
We help celebrate her five million years dying,
old before her time, logrolling her under our feet,
counting our enemies off the other side,
our enemies counting on time to catch up.
    But it keeps its lead
the thing we call mother.
It turns to the moon
her prodigal lover
back again for her periods of unease
cleansing out her womb with tides that smash down
all we can build or be
without her help.
    In spite of all our needs

we do help at her labors.
We deliver bodies to fertilize the body we fight over.
We die to make bodies count for something,
to control the places of slaughter
     that the old terror we still call Mother
     in the earth wind and water
     intended as fields of praise.

Robin Behn

To Rise, So Suddenly

for Phil Mark

If it feels at all like going up in smoke—the fire
all around you so each sound you make
stokes it, each inhaling
burns you deeper—
then I think I came close once in a small church
in New London where we sang in black robes
to a packed house at noon:
you laid rungs in the air with your hands
and we climbed up to an airy cathedral
that you led us into and into
till I felt the choir ring through me,
my weak torso swaying, my small voice the clapper and
part of the bell. . . .

Phil, the man who killed you was driving home
from your concert, still giddy
on brightness he felt from within. They say
his weak heart had stopped before;
he should have been resting, not out by himself
to hear his whole life filled
with forgiveness, measure by measure. His blood
started climbing high in his chest and his heart,
that *so* wanted this, shuddered
and closed on it. I
still want you to lift up your arms, to keep
the last chord sounding forte forever
though we're out of breath,
though time can't be sung back,
though a dead man driving is past being wrong,
though I am too late now to give you these words—
this grief, this disbelief, this vain applause.

Robert Bly

Prayer Service in an English Church

Looking at the open page of the psalm book,
I see a ghostly knot floating in the paper!

Circles within circles on the page, floating,
showing that a branch once lived there!

Looking at the knot long and long,
I hear the priest call on the Saviour to come again.

The old around me keep on singing . . .
If the Saviour is a branch, how can he come again?

And the last day . . .
the whispers we will make from the darkening pillow . . .

Philip Booth

This Day After Yesterday

Robert Trail Spence Lowell (1917–1977)

I

This day after yesterday.

Morning rain small on the harbor,
nothing that's not gray.

I heard at Hooper's, taking the Plymouth in
for brakes. Out from behind
his rolltop desk, Ken said, "*Ra*dio says
a *col*league of yours died. Yessir,
*died. Lo*well. Wasn't he your friend?"

Yesterday blazed, the Bay full of spindrift and sun.
If you'd looked down from your Ireland plane
I could have shared you twelve seals upriver,
seven heron in Warm Cove, and
an early evening meteor.
                    If I'd said such portents,
you would have flattened me with prepschool repartee,
your eyes owl'd out:
                    "And a poet up a fir tree . . ."

II

That's how friendship went.

At least this summer,
this last summer:
                    home,
almost home.

Ulysses come up over the beachstones,
shuffling with terrible age. We hugged and
parted, up the picnic field,
lugging tens of summers.

[15]

III

You wanted women, mail, praise.
What men thought of what you'd conquered.
Beyond the irony of fame, the honor due
to how a poet suffers: the brilliance of first drafts,
the strophe tinker'd into shape, a life
in twelve right lines come almost whole.
You were voluntarily committed: you sweat out hours
to half-know what the day's poems came to.

Who knows what they did? Or,
by your dying, have?
                    Who knows what word
                    you were bringing home?
                    You, bridging marriages,
                    Ulysses into Queens and through.

                    An almost final draft
                    for your collected life,
                    your unrevisable last poem.

        IV

You were a trying man, God knows.
Over drinks, or after, your wit mauled,
twice life sized: like your heroic mattress-chest,

Manic, you were brutal. The brightest boy
in school, the school's most cruel monitor,
you wrenched skin, or twisted arms, as if

Caligula were just. Of those who never made
a team, you were Captain; to them, lifelong,
you were Boston-loyal. Guilt in excess

was your subject, not your better nature.
For sheer guts you had no peer. Sane,
you almost seemed God's gentlest creature.

        V

Jesus, how death gets to us . . .

On the Common, just this week,
they've jacked up Harriet Winslow's house,
all the front sills gone.

And on the sea-side of the Barn
you wrote in, the bulkhead
finally gave way to the tide.

And then the giving-way you,
like Agee, never got to write:
a poet in a New York cab . . .

VI

Weighed by your dying,
Cal, I find myself

much wanting. How could
I dread you less, or

love you more? Left
time, I try to write

old summers back, as if
you'd never maddened

my perspective. More
in misery than love,

I have your life
by heart. Without you,

I am easier and less:
the planet grays,

the village rot
you left eats through

another step, the Bay
that was our commonplace

is flatter . . .

VII

Everything about me
sags: my body tells

my disbelief its
own mortal story.

I meant to write
a different poem:

>   *A seal to tides.*
>   *A heron lifted off.*
>   *A meteor.*

No. If poems
can be believed,

better how
time conjugates:

>   *day by day,*
>   *day after day,*
>   *this day after yesterday . . .*

a dog with flattened
ears, lying on

old dung, lifts
his muzzle, the lame

best that he can,
to welcome his

old master
home.

>   *May all such ghosts attend*
>   *your spirit now. May it,*
>   *with them, be lighter.*

Andrea Hollander Budy

Pigs

It is not the wolf
but his howl in the hollow wind

they fear. His mouth is a great cave
and that howl the master of it—

that sound calling like the night,
calling what is dark to its vacant center.

Straw by straw, stick by stick,
brick by solid brick, there is no way

to keep that sound from entering.
But try. Move in together, give birth,

have other kinds of dreams. Sleep
with a light turned on, with cotton in your ears.

And by the evening fire tell the stories
of your ancestors. Tell how clever they were,

how they tempted the Devil from the skins
of the innocent. How they burned Him

from those useless lives: Catholics, Jews,
witches, saints. And with fire like this.

With fire like this.

Kathryn Stripling Byer

All Hallows Eve

I go by taper of cornstalk,
the last light of fields wreathed in woodsmoke,
to count the hens left in the chickenhouse
raided by wild dogs and foxes.
Our rooster crows far up the hillside
where three piles of rocks mark the graves
of nobody I ever knew.
Let their ghosts eat him!
Each year they grow hungrier,
wanting the squash run to seed in our garden,
the tough spikes of okra. Tonight while the moon
lays her face on the river and begs
for a lovesong, they'll come down the mountain
to steal the last apples I've gathered.

They'll stand at the window and ask us
for whom is that buttermilk set on the table?
That platter of cold beans?
They know we will pay them no heed.
It's the wind, we will say,
watching smoke sidle out of the fireplace,
or hearing the cellar door rattle.

No wonder they go away
always complaining how little we living
have learned, on our knees
every night asking God for a clean heart,
a pure spirit. Spirit? They kick
up the leaves round the silent house.
What good is spirit without hands for walnut
to stain, without ears for the river
to fill up with promises? What good,
they whisper, returning to nothing, what good
without tongue to cry out to the moon,
"Thou hast ravished my heart, O my sister!"

Michael Cadnum

A Dislike for Flowers

Sometimes in this summer of hydrangeas and blowzy
pastel flowers like them it is too
hot to love flowers, too bright, and
all of us want to go down to the
creek and stand shielding our eyes
while bombers from the air-force base

bank, thundering in a quiet way
like the digestion of a horse. Flowers:
easy promise. Easy fulfillment.
And even the bored mistrust this
looseness and crave the hard
straight cold of the stone

shelf under the peat-black
water, the knife
under the arched
foot like a lover pretending

to hurt, hurting
in the sunlight clawed by leaves.

Fred Chappell

Earthsleep

It is the bottomless swoon of never forgetting.

It is the foul well of salvation.

It is the skin of eternity like a coverlet.

It is a tree of fire with tongues of wind.

It is the grandfather lying in earth and the father digging,
The mother aloft in air, the grandmother sighing.

It is the fire that eats the tree of fire.

It is Susan in the hand of sleep a new creature.

I am a new creature born thirty-five years to this earth
Of jarring elements, its fractuous hold
On the man and woman brings earth to bloodmouth.
                            Here where I find
I am I founder.
                Lord Lord
Let this lost dark not.

Who's used?
Who's not scrawled upon
By the wilderness hand of
Earth and fire and water and air?

How simple simple blessèd simple.

It is the fathomless noon that blossoms after midnight,
And daybreak at the margin of the oaks
Begins to sculpt our sleeping bodies
In the wimpled bed.

What shapes may we take now
Where destiny uncurls its roots of fire?

Let it then be flesh that we take on
That I may see you
Cool in time and blonde as this fresh daybreak.

No one no one sleeps apart
Or rises separate
In the burning river of this morning
That earth and wind overtake.

The way the light rubs upon this planet
So do I press to you,

Susan   Susan

The love that moves the sun and other stars
The love that moves itself in light to loving
Flames up like dew

Here is the earliest morning of the world.

Kelly Cherry

Letter to a Censor

Simply, one must imagine what has been lost:
The light along the edge of the lake gone dark

As death, leftover leaves
Crumbled into mulch and ground

Underfoot, a cry
Like a bird's or a child's, imprinting the waxsoft sky

With its echo, mind with memory—
Lost, lost. One must imagine

What has been, what has been lost
Between the third line and the fifth

Between the first page and the third
Between the third envelope and the fifth

With its official *Recommandé*.
And night eats up the flowers of the day.

One must imagine what has been
Lost in the mouth of the censor

Swallowed
Shat from the bowels of the censor

And lost. Lost. Perhaps one lives somewhere which is not
Where the one whom that one loves lives,

And then one must imagine the shortest distance
Between these two points

A line,
Deleted.

Perhaps one whom one has loved in August
Is forbidden to write in November, and his words appear at night

Like stars in the dome of the brain's planetarium.
Or perhaps it is still later, and the scene shifts

As scenes do,
Wordlessly.

The mind drops heavily into sleep, the undersides of the lids
Are painted with bright, moving pictures—

We are dancing a minuet in the mind.
The great gate strains against its lock in the noisy night wind.

The lake's blackness is rolling over and under its winking whiteness
And the lights in the mansion glow like white-gold winter stars.

Simply, there is a storm picking up and strewing all things before it
                                                like confetti
And words are scattered into silence like frightened animals, lost,

And love and friendship are separated, lost,
Summer has become the orphan of the seasons, abandoned, lost,

And music is drowned on the wind.

We are dancing a minuet in the mind.
One must imagine.

Kevin Clark

Widow Under a New Moon

I

Evening
has overtaken the parlor.
I cannot see my mother
sitting on the porch,
but I know exactly how
she holds herself, knees
tight against her chest.

II

There is
the story of my father
and me playing catch
in the street. We would
throw high flies to each
other as dusk came on.
In time, we would not see
the ball until an instant
from our faces, when
all luck was reflex.

Once, mightily, he threw
the ball to the moonless
night and I moved closer
to him, gauging its point
of return. There was
a long pause, then her voice.

III

I get up
from the rocker and go
to the door. I ask
her if she'll be coming

in soon, would
she like a cup of tea.
She does not answer
but asks
if we ever found the ball
that night. I tell her
what I have repeated
a thousand times. No,
it must have landed
in a sewer or an open drain.

IV

At this
moment, I am slicing
lemon for her tea.
I can hear her setting
china on the table,
the delicate clicks
freezing me in my place.
Soon she will take
a single taste of pie,
a few inaudible sips
of chamomile. Carefully,
she will avoid my eyes.
Then, in strained
monotone, she will claim
that he never believed
the ball landed
in the sewer, that he
believed it was a sign.
I will place my cup
on the saucer
and inhale the sweet steam.
And tonight, finally,
perhaps I will say
yes, he might have been right

and she will be gone.

Peter Cooley

Ararat

This is the room where summer ends.
This is the view, a single window
opening to evening: banks of clouds,
shivering to be called down quickly,
step forward, naked, to greet me.

How beautiful each is, assuming
animal form on the lawn
never known before, with beaks & tusks
silver, their feathers, fluttering, gold.
Quivering, they pair off, pair off

till I wonder if the ark has docked tonight
for me. I am not ready yet
though darkness falls from the air
& I have dreamed of this. I've got to pack,
I've got to be wished well by somebody

familiar. The animals are darkening,
calling. They are wading the dark, thrashing.
And now their ivory fetlocks, their horns,
demand an answer going down, *Are you coming
before the waves close over us, are you?*

So. This is my night to leave
carrying nothing, the wind between my eyes,
no one to clear the room of me
or to lie down with me even once.
No one saying the dark is not enough.

Stephen Corey

Bread

for Susan

There will be bread no matter what,
so you choose to mourn with flour
powdering your hairline,
with your hands shredded by strings of dough.
You can dream the desert of Moses,
the beehive ovens of Africa,
the softest *croissants* of erotic days—
anything but this chilling house,
the death of your closest friend.
You mourn through the beat of your hands' kneading,
for the unbroken history of bread
is neither accident nor wonder,
but the survival of simplicity:
bread was our purest creation,
flour transformed by water and fire.

Someone watching from across the yard
or high above the reddening autumn trees
could not know what special grain you breed—
the sour tang of rye, the sweet heaviness of white—
but would know each grows from grief,
that single soil we always walk.

As the smooth loaves warm and swell
under the dampened cloth, and the oven's heat
drifts to adjoining rooms, you give yourself
a moment to believe in miracles.
But your aching hands recall you
to the work this day has been,
while the dried and cracking film of dough
stiffens your fingers until they seem,
themselves, the residue of failure.
In the burning water from the faucet,

you scrub your skin and scrape your nails
as if somehow they could come to match
the rising gold of the oven's loaf.

But the full beauty of bread
resides in its consumption,
and you know the threat of weeks to come:
you will raise a hand to point directions,
or you will circle your lover's neck
until your hand comes close to your face:
and there, buried beneath the nail
like a shard of your own bones,
the last dried speck of dough—
the savior that cracks your heart.

Carl Dennis

The List

How the frail, shimmering hollyhocks
Share in a bloom that's deathless and invisible—
That was the question that kept the students awake
Chewing their quills in the old school,
Staring at the blank pages of diaries.
How much simpler for me to make my list
Of every beautiful, dying thing I come across.
Rainy West Delham Street gets a line
And rain-washed Ellicott Elementary School
With the puddles in the schoolyard,
And the sunrise on the flags of the car lot,
And the cars themselves, dozing in the shadows.

As for the beautiful moments,
Why should I wait around anymore
For the sidewalk to part like the Red Sea
Or the painter's ladder to fill with angels,
Visions that prove the world a dream?
The moments that make the world seem real
Are all I need now. I can add to my list
The foggy morning when the children next door
Woke me with a trumpet fanfare.
And I'll add this evening too, as I stroll with my friend
Down to the dock, talking about the shabby movie,
What exactly went wrong with it.
We get the problem of ugly art beautifully clear
By the time we pause at the tracks
To count the boxcars, close to a hundred,
All sporting the rust I noticed as a boy.
They've almost dropped their pretense of utility.
Their rattling by again is part of a ritual
To make me feel at home, I say to myself,
Borrowing arrogance from the old school
That believed in beauty waiting in another world.

[31]

William Dickey

Windows

are needed to put a frame around the landscape
which otherwise escapes into its own business.
Picture frames isolate what is the picture
from what is not the picture, and permit identification.
All these rectangular or square spaces
are similar, so is the printed page.

Open a book, the left page and the right page are equal.
The left brain and the right brain are equal.
This balance is significant, cities balance around squares
with a single warrior erect to the tip of his bronze sword.
He is historical because he is in his frame.
He is an agreement our brains have reached about him.

At its extreme, painting can dispense with objects
and see only the balance, the fact of containment
rather than things contained. That square information.
Now both the emperor and his clothes are needless.
Looking at an equation about emperors
their numbers vanish, and only an equal sign remains.

We can look in at the window, or out the window.
Windows are intended for safety between in and out.
In Amsterdam, the whores sit behind windows.
It is unnecessary to know what they are thinking.
They are there to be equal to what we are thinking.
If there were no glass, we would not know they are whores.

I have only met you, and already I find myself
thinking of taking photographs: your face,
your body to the waist, these civil squares
thinking to make you still, thinking to tame you,
thinking to look out or in at you through my square window,
through which I have watched so often these small elegies.

Wayne Dodd

Sometimes Music Rises

Above the snuffle and scurry
of one's own
minor blood, the neck-snapping thunk
a grouse makes as it startles up
into a window, its fanned
tail feathers quivering
with color—brown, ocher, russet—
the driftwood it lies beside smoothed
by rocks
to the curve of a bird's wing.

Or on earth personal
as breathing, a garage leans
back through summer
toward the sound, not
of saw and axe
in the act of tree fall,
but of wood bees droning
above the private
gloom everyone who slumps
suddenly to the floor
turns into.
"Is it true?" a father asks
in disbelief,
and wood dust falls
from the rafters like denials
of the future.

And what if today someone you
named lingers
beside a stream
and hears, in the great
silence around her, cold
water promising nothing

but itself, the curve
her arm makes among the rocks
a mere accident
of time and weather?

Of Sitting Bear

(from *The General Mule Poems*)

Hoka hey, Lakotas, Sioux warriors used to shout
before riding into battle: *It's a good day
to die.* Comanche braves must have said it
every morning before breakfast.
Now the Comanches I don't miss much,
and the Plains Indian may not have been
the noblest human ever to walk
or ride the surface of the earth, but I say
it does take something fine
to make a man, old and sick and huddled
beneath a blanket, patiently, mile
after mile in an open wagon, strip
the flesh away from his wrists
with his teeth, until at last the manacles slide
from his hands and he attacks
and attacks and attacks the guarding soldiers
till they shoot him finally
to death, there on the road
to prison, because it was,
he knew, a bad day for Sitting Bear
to be captured, but a good day to die.

William Doreski

Thanksgiving, Growing Older

Cigars droop in sickly fingers.
Thanksgiving Day sighs through the house
like a child's inflatable toy.
Primed with highballs, early risers
sway onto the porch to puzzle
the blood weather face to face.
The old men keep puffing, but
cigars can't relight themselves,
the turkeys can't reclaim their heads,
the Indians can't retract
the welcome they gave the Pilgrims.
In the past the winter's breath
had sucked the clouds to bits of string
by now; the elms clanked their chain mail,
the wind had sown its flint. Uncles,
now long dead, tuned in football games
while my aunts sampled chocolate pies.
But here in Boston my neighbors
stumble in too late for New Year's,
tugging at limp faces caught
between this mirror and the next.
Here is no real shift of season:
just one matched set of silences
to fit the gaps in the traffic.
Heart attacks are more common
on holidays like this, when sand
creeps in to fill the blind spots,
when all the secrets we thought
were trustworthy parade naked
in the cold, shocking no one. . . .
Let the dead Indians whisper
over a hundred polished birds,

a thousand stubbed-out cigars;
let the sand rise in our sleep and
catch in a million throats——the word
of apology we've misspelled
as thanks to our embittered gods.

Rita Dove

Receiving the Stigmata

There is a way to enter a field
empty-handed, your shoulder
behind you and air tightening.

The kite comes by itself,
a spirit on a fluttering string.

Back when people died for
the smallest reasons, there was
always a field to walk into.
Simple men fell to their knees
below the radiant crucifix
and held out their palms

in relief. Go into the field
and it will reward. Grace

is a string growing straight
from the hand. Is
the hatchet's shadow on the
rippling green.

Stephen Dunn

Enough Time

for Lyn Harrison

I used to think:
out of small things, a lifetime.
Out of a night full of stars,
a universe. But tonight
I want to pick, deny,
believe only in the irrational
pull upwards
to where the gods lie
in their spacious graves.
Out of small things, perhaps,
fragments, a scattering.
Out of a night full of stars,
one that falls
seemingly in our direction.
Enough. All that's falling
is the temperature. And the world
is down here in neighborhoods
where the trash piles up
and I've danced
and, in time, will dance again.
I know the moon, this awful night,
is saying something
uplifting to the sea.
I know starfish and sharks
exist without contradiction.
      Lyn dead at thirty-one
who allowed me to compliment her
on her thinness when only she knew.
Lyn, who had enough time
to be appalled and fascinated.

Because We Are Not Taken Seriously

Some night I wish they'd knock
on my door, the government men,
looking for the poem of simple truths
recited and whispered among the people.
And when all I give them is silence
and my children are exiled
to the mountains, my wife forced
to renounce me in public,
I'll be the American poet
whose loneliness, finally, is relevant,
whose slightest movement
ripples cross-country.

And when the revolution frees me,
its leaders wanting me to become
"Poet of the Revolution," I'll refuse
and keep a list of their terrible reprisals
and all the dark things I love
which they will abolish.
With the ghost of Mandelstam
on one shoulder, Lorca
on the other, I'll write the next poem,
the one not even a bullet can stop
once it's in the air, singing.

Charles Edward Eaton

Biography of a Still Life

A green bottle, a gray pipe, a very stiff and moral-looking tablecloth:
Somewhere in this limpid combination an abstraction enters—
You retreat, and say the pipe is precisely colored like a moth,

The bottle, a lizard's skin melted in the very hottest fire;
You take back the moral, and say the cloth is plainly white—
If you do not want the picture singed, why put it on the pyre?

So once again: the bottle is pristine, the pipe astute, the cloth demure.
It will not do to keep them focused, fanatically, all alone,
Though we allude, and, no doubt, rightly should, to how we mean
                                                    to keep them pure.

Compromise: Admit into the bottle some absinthe-looking sort of wine;
An ember in the pipe, a stainlike shadow on the cloth—
In any manner that you move, you make a motion toward design.

A bottle, a pipe, and cloth, and you are powerfully committed:
An enormous choking, throbbing world pushes up a sea of causes,
                                                    claims—
To what can just these vulnerable three judiciously be fitted?

It is a loose, loose thing, therefore, this clarity and light,
The slightly lascivious green, cerebral gray, the rigid cloth—
You heard the picture talking like yourself, heard it clearly,
        and then, not quite.

Gary Eddy

Desire

The first weather of spring gathers and slopes
a spruce like a horse's neck under the weight
of wind that wants everything flat, except itself.

And wind will be the only thing with shape—so much
shape that no one can tell what it looks like,
everything moving at once. So is it the maker?

Or what follows the maker, naming the made? Or what
carries the bells and trembles inside them?
Or what blows this page away unread?

It holds the seagull in place who flaps like a blizzard
and gales across the promising land, pulling up the present
like a bead of sweat from a wheat shock, and now it bends

the grass on the hills that could be clouds that could be
waves with sparse veins and hair, saying *never die*
even as it dies here, where my body ends, and yours.

Lynn Emanuel

You Tell Me

You tell me you're the stranger in bad weather,
I'm the girl hitching east in your dream.
You tell me I think it's beautiful:
the storm approaching on the solid body of wheat,
clouds knotting the light
and each root connecting in the furrows
until the acres tear under the thresher
as easily as old silk.
Which is not your freedom.
You have chosen to see how the sun is blank as a tack,
and we come past Leadville lonely with our fights
on roads where people die each winter
parked like lovers in their cars.
You try to explain about the workers,
barges, coal, pipe, some small town
where the dead have their churches and we stop
to watch a seizure of light in an open door.
The only thing that bores me more than dreams is God.
I am slightly drunk, a young widow
with a derringer, riding out of Wichita
toward Pittsburgh—all those broken homes,
the smell of sulphur and the fire
where men exhaust themselves in shifts,
you tell me.

John Engels

The Harbor

My shadow swims before me
over the dry, fiery soils
until at last it cools itself

on the stone wharves, stretches
over the sea which has crept inshore
to become the harbor,

at its edges golden
with long drifts
of pollen, thickening

into wracks and stoneworts,
into the slow mass of the stone itself,
the land rising behind me

as if the sea had stolidly
heaved itself up
into the long swells of foothills,

mountains, into the whole cresting ridge
of the continent which breaks
to the north, bears

down on me, slowly
ebbs, at my feet
becomes the harbor, swells

and subsides
like breathing.

Mark A. R. Facknitz

Topography

The line between the city and the
wilderness is broad and indistinct,
a place for rich men and the very poor.
Mad dogs prefer this last zone
to the middle class's second circle
of bungalows and shopping malls.
Wastelanders need their insecurity;
they love the openness, the ditch
filled with trash and wildflowers,
the rusted car body that sprouts
saplings and herniates a chain-link
fence topped with concertina wire,
or the big field gouged over
with tracks of motorcycles where
at night the mad dogs and coyotes
hunt and eat each other.
Often the middlers spread and
overtake such land, but never wholly.
A suburban gardener will rototill
the bones of a murdered man, or a
coyote's prints will appear in wet cement.
Always there is an insolent monument.
An old woman's shack, henhouse, and
acre of box elders and dying poplars
cannot be bought and so insult
physicians, lawyers, and civil engineers
who, with swimming pools, triple
garages, mugho pines, and floodlights,
try to hex the savage civilization
that gives up the ground but not the causes
of the defeated and the mighty.

Alice Friman

The Reckoning

We meet tonight to pass the point of blame
dealt out like a marked deck
sticky from past games and fingers.
We meet in the hole of last week's fire
scorched grass, scrub. Two bloodhounds
sniffing at the blackened stones.

On a nearby twig, a mantis
mates and mangles in the same clutch.
It is an old confrontation, an ancient fire:
the horse-drawn gift of Greeks
wrapped in the ribboned knot of Helen's legs,
the wet slick that licks the scrotal sac
oils the flare and rages.
The pyre of Troy was struck
when the bed of Paris heaved with heat
running fire down the sweet sheets
scenting blood with lavender.

No wonder of it:
The angel's sword was struck in Eden.
It roots where it fell, blazing in orchards.
And we, promised by blossoms, run gathering
bushels of cinders, black and still as nuns.

Robert Frost

From a Milkweed Pod

Calling all butterflies of every race
From source unknown but from no special place
They ever will return to all their lives,
Because unlike the bees they have no hives,
The milkweed brings up to my very door
The theme of wanton waste in peace and war
As it has never been to me before.
And so it seems a flower's coming out
That should if not be talked then sung about.
The countless wings that from the infinite
Make such a noiseless tumult over it
Do no doubt with their color compensate
For what the drab weed lacks of the ornate.
For drab it is its fondest must admit.
And yes, although it is a flower that flows
With milk and honey, it is bitter milk,
As anyone who ever broke its stem
And dared to taste the wound a little knows.
It tastes as if it might be opiate.
But whatsoever else it may secrete,
Its flowers' distilled honey is so sweet
It makes the butterflies intemperate.
There is no slumber in its juice for them.
One knocks another off from where he clings.
They knock the dyestuff off each other's wings—
With thirst on hunger to the point of lust.
They raise in their intemperance a cloud
Of mingled butterfly and flower dust
That hangs perceptibly above the scene.
In being sweet to these ephemerals
The sober weed has managed to contrive
In our three hundred days and sixty-five
One day too sweet for beings to survive.
Many shall come away as struggle worn

And spent and dusted off of their regalia
To which at daybreak they were freshly born
As after one-of-them's proverbial failure
From having beaten all day long in vain
Against the wrong side of a window pane.

But waste was of the essence of the scheme.
And all the good they did for man or god
To all those flowers they passionately trod
Was leave as their posterity one pod
With an inheritance of restless dream.
He hangs on upside down with talon feet
In an inquisitive position odd
As any Guatemalan parakeet.
Something eludes him. Is it food to eat?
Or some dim secret of the good of waste?
He almost has it in his talon clutch.
Where have those flowers and butterflies all gone
That science may have staked the future on?
He seems to say the reason why so much
Should come to nothing must be fairly faced.*

*And shall be in due course

Alice Fulton

Dance Script with Electric Ballerina

Here I am on this ledge again,
my body's five rays singing,
limbering up for another fling
with gravity. It's true,
I've dispensed with some conventions.
If you expected sleeping
beauty sprouting from a rococo
doughnut of tulle, a figurine
fit to top a music box, you might want
your money back. I'll take a get-up
functional as light:
feet bright and precise as eggbeaters,
fingers quick as switch-
blades and a miner's lamp for my tiara.
You've seen kids on Independence Day, waving
sparklers to sketch their initials on the night?
Just so, I'd like to leave a residue
of slash and glide, a trace-
form on the riled air.
Like an action painter, tossing form on space
instead of oil on cloth,
I'm out to disprove the limited
orbit of fingers, swing some double-jointed
miracles, train myself to hover above ground
longer than the pinch of time allowed.

This stingy escarpment leaves so little
room to move!
But perhaps that's for the best. Despite brave talk
of brio and ballon, spectators prefer
gestures that don't endanger
body and soul. Equilibrium
is so soothing—while any strain is a reminder
of the pain that leads to grace:

[48]

muscles clenched like teeth to the shin, swollen
hubs of shoulder, ankle, wrist, and knee,
toes brown as figs from the clobbering
of poundage. In this game, lightness is all.
Here's another trick. When passing the critics
turn sideways to expose less
surface. Think like a knife
against the whetstone sneers: *unsympathetic*
in several minds flat and hollow
at the core shabby too
flaccid polishes off her pirouettes with
too assertive
a flick ragged barbaric hysterical
needs to improve
her landings technique bullies
the audience into paying
attention in short
does not really get around lacking
assurance authority fluency restraint roundness
of gesture something
of the air and manner of those who are ballerinas
by right rather than
assumption: one will say
I'm mildly impressed
by her good line and high extensions.

I can sense the movement
notators' strobe vision
picking the bones of flux into
positions. Can't they see the gulf
between gestures as a chance
to find clairvoyance—
a gift that thrives on fissures
between then and now and when?
If a complex network, a city, say,
could be filmed for a millennium
and the footage shown
so in three hours it woke
from huts to wired shining,

its compressed assembling would be like this
dance: these air patterns
where I distill the scribbling moves
that start at birth
and dissolve in death.

Till then I'm signing space
in leaps angular and brief
as an electrocardiograph's beat.
Now as I settle on an ending
posture: my chest heaves,
joints shift, eyes dart—
and even at a stand-
still, I'm dancing.

Brendan Galvin

Saying Her Name

Women who heard
Pipsissewa
on the lips of dreaming braves
had sufficient tribal grounds
for divorce.

She was so beautiful
no man was allowed to sleep
and remember her,
and when she died for love
this is the flower
that appeared over her grave.

I have been spinning
elaborations
about this low-growing evergreen
for days:
how they gave it
the consolation of her name,

how the flower
seems to hover above meadows,
how the sepals, brewed by lovers
and drunk from a single cup,
ensure fidelity.

I have made all this up
out of a crooked need
to deepen truth:
the last Pamet Indian
lies with his myths
somewhere around here,

and taller than hog cranberry,
in this pine shade beneath
the notice of herbalists,
Pipsissewa grows.

Its flower looks at the ground,
so, in my version,
it remembers. And when
I slip a finger under its chin

and look it in the eye,
someone muffled in me
as in a quilt
steps out saying her name.

Old Map of Barnstable County

It doesn't show
how the cold edge of starlight
pierced woodpiles,

or the boy forking hay
who one afternoon cries out to no one
on the shore of Still Pond
and runs away to sea,

but crawls ashore years later,
to lie under this mapmaker's
pinpoint, which stands for "humane house,"
and gasp white-eyed on the straw floor,
his hands scrabbling his chest
for its breath.

Who would believe,
on this mapmaker's **Atlantic**,
which looks safe as a strip of corduroy,

a schooner is floundering,

and soon heartbreak will walk
the sand roads up hollows
to Mrs. Small, Mrs. Snow, Mrs. Dyer,
sea widows whose lives will go on
in ways the cartographer's black squares
for houses can never explain?

A red dot for each vessel lost
would turn this map
to a rash like scarlet fever,

quick as a camera's shutter
that sea would close over islands,

and the griefs that went by the names
beside the black squares
would move on to other squares,

as on later maps
even the black squares
will have moved on.

James Galvin

A Man's Vocation Is Nobody's Business

Overcome with humility in the American West,
Boys grew up incorruptible in old photographs.
In shirts without collars
They stand next to the year's prize hog,
Thinking into the wind.

Taller than fathers or brothers,
The edges of kitchen doors
In sod houses
Recorded the ambitions of boys to grow

Tall enough to see more of the landscape
As it took its turns for the worse.

From the top of a silo you could see
How the land had a hard time
Just holding up its fences,
Holding out for water, just holding
Back the sage and larkspur.

In Eastern Colorado, old men and boys
Rode the fences together.
Once a year in late summer
They lifted the fencewires to the tops of cedar posts
For the tumbleweeds to blow under.

This is no secret.
The tumbleweed is a bristling genius,
Bound for the edge of the world.

Dan Gerber

In the Winter Dark

The door half open
in a dark hallway, roller-skate
on the stairs, marbles
scattered on the kitchen floor,
hold those impenetrable silences
between father and son
as the two drive home in the winter dark.

Do these smouldering logs, waiting
to be stirred back to flame
become the compulsion to build cathedrals,
pyramids, tombs,
The Great Buried Silos of North Dakota?

The shadow of a man trudges over the field.

One of those logs in the fireplace
suddenly takes off on its own
burning furiously
through a pocket of air.

The light fails so early.
The hemlocks grow heavy.

The shadow drives an image of the man before it.

Gary Gildner

Wheat

Alone up north, soaking this nutty bulgur for supper
I think of wheat and the landscapes of wheat
the furred winter, the hard-kerneled durum, the Turkey
Red smuggled over in the fierce pockets of Mennonites
of einkorn, emmer, and spelt, the ancients on the calendar
near Grandma's moony pie crusts cooling in the window
and her hot biscuits, a spoonful of butter
oozing creamily over their soft loamy interiors

Of whiskey and beer and my Polish uncles, flushed
and tanned on leave from the Army, establishing order
and chaos around the kitchen table, wanting to know
"How many fingers?" and hoisting, toasting, "*Na zdrowie!*"
I think of China and Kansas and Russia
of standing beside a gravel road near everything, near
nothing but rain and wheat and two Appaloosas
all leaning the same wet way

I think of school, of handing over my pickle
and braunschweiger sandwich to the big blond boxer
that stood between me and St. Joseph's, long strings of saliva
hanging down from his bubbled lips, and leaping back, sprawling
watching the sky sneak by under the common witch hazel, lying
belly down on the log bridge over Grandpa's creek, leaning
way over watching my mouth above the swarming shiners
trying to shout "*Psia Krew!*" like he did when the bull

Got stubborn or the cow kicked over the milk, learning years
later it meant "Dog's Blood!" and wondering why *that*
made Grandma cross herself, wondering what the shiny pink
lump was on the neck of the old farmer kneeling bent
and nut-wrinkled in the front pew of their little Standish church
An egg, Grandma whispered, and I believed her, remembering

the raw potato Grandpa carried in his pocket to help
loosen his stiff leg, but wondering how he got it

Under his skin like that, I think of cutting open a cock's belly
and finding the mush of wheat mixed with buckshot
of nest and nide and nye which collect pheasants
of cast and cete and mute which collect hawks, badgers, and hounds
of leash which collects foxes
of all the ragtail information I've collected
that will never make me rich
of the woolly itch on the back of my neck

From the scapular Grandma gave me, the Holy Family patch
at one end, the Bleeding Heart at the other, one of them dangling
past my belt and getting in the way when I had to pee fast
my back and belly prickly with hay and sweat
of running plenty ahead of
Grandpa and Prince and Nelly and the hay cutter
my shins red and sore from kicking the cut stems
following beside the unmowed edge with my burlap bag flying

Jumping over mice and garter snakes all snipped up
in the cutter's wake, over the sudden bright scatterings
of newborn rabbits I didn't catch and run with to the sweet
bee-stippled orchard, among the windfallen Goldens, the spongy
snows, and release, I think of the cold sweaty jar
of spring water waiting in the shade, of lifting it
with both hands to my mouth, inhaling aromas
of iron and cellar and wet gravel scooped

Fresh from the stream bed, of wishing
I had a mustache sparkling with drops of this water
to wipe with the back of my wrist, of pulling off the salt-
slick harnesses and slapping the horses' shoulders and flanks
letting my hand linger on their foamy hindquarters
of cantering easily beside them down to the trout's black pool
the fine hairs on my face flat on the water, collecting bubbles
my muzzle in deep, like theirs, for a long drink

I think of swinging down from the barn's full mow, the rope
burning my palms, the fork overhead with its three prongs
long as a man's arm tight against the pulley, descending
through dust- and feather-flecked sheets of fading light
and hearing my young uncle howling from the roof of the granary
hearing a late killdeer's last noisy shriek and hearing
my uncle again under the close and giddy first star of evening
howling he was stone-blind-gone-to-hell drunk on wheat wine
and what did the damn pigs and chickens and cows, what did
    the damn bull think of that

David Graham

Landscape of Domestic Life

The bacon was carved thin
as a lesson, to be taught
by nervous elders
whose every movement
became a skill,
like calming animals.

Some paychecks were good
for buying more checks, fathers
using sons to make grandsons,
pitching themselves
lifelong into that debt.
Sticky butterknives passed

hand to hand down the long table,
still our breakfast smalltalk
revolved always
around the silent center—
fish your own hole,
fish your own hole.

For children the curfew horn meant
the helpless have no business
being stupid. So we found our way home
across unlit yards,
through pried cellar windows,
to pillows asleep in our forms.

Jorie Graham

Jackpot

Halfway through Illinois on the radio
they are giving away jackpots.
I can hear them squeal as they win.
Luck in this landscape lies flat
as if to enter the ground and add to it as well.
You can see its traces, milkweed caught in the fences,
the sheen on the new grass
that could be sunshine or white paint.
But the brushstroke is visible.
We wouldn't believe anything we saw without it—

the brown, the green, the rectangle, the overpass.
I believe now that sorrow
is our presence in this by default.
In a little while I hope there will be shadows,
the houses and these trees trying to bury half of themselves.
This could be your lucky day,
the day the roof is put on the house,
and the willows once again resemble trees,
and the bridge falls in, making the river once again
sufficiently hard to cross.

Haying

Some meanings move
the way my neighbor has to move,
round and round,
trying to give irregular and interrupted ground
its even wave, its
permanent.
Some have to move this way, in heat and the dust
of their own
making.
For some terrains are fixed
in their unevenness,
are beautiful . . .
The man in the next field has perfectly
straight rows, clean ground.
His bales are true.
My man has placed his anywhere he can, between
outcrops and stumps. Where work is done
the forest is held back, we say,
and then—as if we could
see further
where there's less to see—we say he owns
the *clearing*.
Yet his is the place for darkness, I think,
where the crop is a broken
wake. The place
for belief,
that fastening that's done by ripping stitches
out. And love
which is where the farmer
wrenches his machine
to keep one perfect square of useless green
around his house.

Robert Graves

Judgement of Paris

What if Prince Paris, after taking thought,
Had not adjudged the apple to Aphrodite
But, instead, had chosen buxom Hera
Divine defendress of the marriage couch?
What if Queen Helen had been left to squander
Her beauty upon the thralls of Menelaus,
Hector to die unhonoured in his bed,
Penthesileia to hunt a poorer quarry,
The bards to celebrate a meaner siege?
Could we still have found the courage, you and I
To embark together for Cranae
And consummate our no less fateful love?

Debora Greger

The Second Violinist's Son

You grow up with music
but what do you know about it?
The minor third my mother used
to call my name, the whole step
of the phoebe's cry—those
recognitions were in the blood.

My father, no talkative man,
shut himself in the bedroom
nights with his violin. Did he
make it speak? What did he play?
It was nothing I could hum—
a melody turned upside down.

I was concerned with the details
of growing up. Years later,
trying to sit still at a concert,
I was shaken, hard, by something
familiar—my father's part,
just under the orchestra's surface.

It was something like the plain
warp on which a complicated weft
is threaded. Or the shadowy figures
in the background of a relief
that fix the illusion of depth.
This thick layered sound

must have been what he listened for,
practicing. What I heard now
was a kind of completion he found
only outside himself.

Jeanine Hathaway

The Name of God Is

simple as the attraction
of nipple and mouth,
the spring songs
of everything seasonal.
Expansive as bread.
Creatures of a silent life
store it outside the interruption
of syllables (as mountain, desert,
deepest water). Beasts are born
with it hidden like an extra cord
in the voicebox. The name of God
is a great cave in which
we say our own names and
our own names return to us
round as song; full of snow;
striking.

Hunt Hawkins

The Prejohn

Last night at the movie theater,
going to relieve myself,
I kept thinking what a hard day
Adam must have had
when he was obliged to name all those animals:
kangaroo, porcupine, protozoa, drosophila, and on and on.
That must be why so many things
remain unnamed;
for example, the little room you enter
before you get to the bathroom.
I paused there, puzzled, pondering—
and hoping no one would come in and get the wrong impression.
What's the purpose of this room? You say
it's so outsiders of the different gender
don't catch any untoward sights,
but clearly we don't need a whole room for that—
just a crook or partition.
Why have prejohns
when we don't have precars or prekitchens?
I examined the room carefully.
It had bright lights, flowered wallpaper, white moldings.
I've had friends who lived in worse places than this!
And think of the thousands of prejohns across the country,
empty, going to waste.
We should at least put in shelves
and use them to store jams and jellies.
Or they could house refugees
from countries less fortunate and democratic than our own.
Or we could chain a prisoner in each one.
That way, not only would we relieve prison overcrowding,
but we'd provide a warning against crime
to every citizen going to take a whiz.
But something's wrong here—

it's the room itself we should get rid of.
We've all become Greta Garbos
in our quest for privacy.
We've become islands, not part of the main.
Why do we even need a bathroom
to go to the bathroom?
Shouldn't we be more like Adam's animals,
innocent and free, urinating in the wind,
defecating in the fields,
returning what we don't need
to great Nature from which it came?
O, yes, yes, shouldn't we be more like the French?

Anthony Hecht

The Feast of Stephen

I

The coltish horseplay of the locker room,
Moist with steam of the tiled shower stalls,
With shameless blends of civet, musk and sweat,
Loud with the cap-gun snapping of wet towels
Under the steel-ribbed cages of bare bulbs,
In some such setting of thick basement pipes
And janitorial realities
Boys for the first time frankly eye each other,
Inspect each others' bodies at close range,
And what they see is not so much another
As a strange, possible version of themselves,
And all the sparring dance, adrenal life,
Tense, jubilant nimbleness, is but a vague,
Busy, unfocused ballet of self-love.

II

If the heart has its reasons, perhaps the body
Has its own lumbering sort of carnal spirit,
Felt in the tingling bruises of collision,
And known to captains as *esprit de corps*.
What is this brisk fraternity of timing,
Pivot and lobbing arc, or indirection,
Mens sana in men's sauna, in the flush
Of health and toilets, private and corporal glee,
These fleet caroms, *pliés* and genuflections
Before the salmon-leap, the leaping fountain
All sheathed in glistening light, flexed and alert?
From the vast echo-chamber of the gym,
Among the scumbled shouts and shrill of whistles,
The bounced basketball sound of a leather whip.

III

Think of those barren places where men gather
To act in the terrible name of rectitude,
Of acned shame, punk's pride, muscle or turf,
The bully's thin superiority.
Think of the *Sturm-Abteilungs Kommandant*
Who loves Beethoven and collects Degas,
Or the blond boys in jeans whose narrowed eyes
Are focused by some hard and smothered lust,
Who lounge in a studied mimicry of ease,
Flick their live butts into the standing weeds,
And comb their hair in the mirror of cracked windows
Of an abandoned warehouse where they keep
In darkened readiness for their occasion
The rope, the chains, handcuffs and gasoline.

IV

Out in the rippled heat of a neighbor's field,
In the kilowatts of noon, they've got one cornered.
The bugs are jumping, and the burly youths
Strip to the waist for the hot work ahead.
They go to arm themselves at the dry-stone wall,
Having flung down their wet and salty garments
At the feet of a young man whose name is Saul.
He watches sharply these superbly tanned
Figures with a swimmer's chest and shoulders,
A miler's thighs, with their self-conscious grace,
And in between their sleek, converging bodies,
Brilliantly oiled and burnished by the sun,
He catches a brief glimpse of bloodied hair
And hears an unintelligible prayer.

William Heyen

Plague Sermon

Some were for fires—not coal,
but wood fires for the city,
whole forests of fires
carted into the city,
some for the turpentine effluvia
of fir and cedar, some for wetted
pine billowing life-saving smoke, some
for oak's skin-basting
pustule-drying heat. No
use. What is the wood
under your breastbone?

Mornings and evenings
the wagons made their rounds:
Bring out your dead. We did,
the funerals becoming so many
we could not toll the bell,
mourn, weep, wear aught
but black, or make coffins.
Grass returned to the desolate streets,
wind shattered windows
in empty houses; the stricken
left their beds by night to make
moonlit silhouettes of antic gesture,
laugh, speak to trees or dogs,
reign as king or queen of Britain
for an hour, or curse the church,
or leap into the Thames.
What is your faithful song?
Bring out your dead. And we did.

And you who hear this,
centuries hence,

but under aegis of the same
circular Providence,
you who harbor the pestilence within
where only the soul's light,
the Lord's warm breath
under your lungs can save you,
bring out your dead.

Jonathan Holden

Cutting Beetle-Blighted Ponderosa Pine

In one week we dismantled
the little old country of the sky—
that wonderful colored
map. At anchor in its blue
harbors, between civilizations,
the big clouds would ride.
With my chainsaw I opened
tracts of raw sky, cleared
until the last land in sight,
our single pier, our outpost
was one grandfather
of a tree. I chipped at
its trunk, chipped,
scaling bark-scabs off until
the hatchet skimmed wet
meat. But there were
those bluish-gray streaks
in it. I kept the saw shaking
and digging until I struck
the nerve. The tree
shivered, its spine groaning
in its throat.
When it let out a deep
croak and, shuddering,
sank into the dust, the rest
of the sky—nothing
to hold it back, sky without
a profile—rolled over
my head, more sky than **anyone**
can handle.

John Hollander

Monuments

for Natalie Charkow

Start here: something has exhaled this marble and moved
On, itself a kind of wind. Yet what blows among
The carvings now and the polished tablets can feel
Nothing of the stone it touches, which feels nothing
Of air. And could it grab your hand and lead you toward
A momentary splendor—against the sky soaked
In blue a Great Spangled Fritillary hanging
Among the white tombs—this would have been a picture
Only of the remembrance of connection,
A quick fable of fragile wings alighting on
Heavy slabs sunk in the darkness of earth, telling
No tall truth, flourishing in no parable field.

No more to worry then at the dry leaf blowing
Against whatever text has been cut into stone.
A plaything of the daughters of marble and the
Descendants of wind, it should urge no eye to rest
In mid-journey upon its marginalia.
For in the conditional truth of turf, here lies
Stone, whose inscriptions keep being sure of what was
Not, by way of hedging about what was: bodies
Now grounded below pain who lay above in life
Sleeping in beds of white, dreaming the blank, black ground,
Bodies who, when pain came in such a sleep, would grow
A limb of hurt to be the place where pain would lie.

And what members of joy grew up at the sweet touch
Of heart laying sure hands on body from within
Are pictured only now in shapes under the grass,
Always dreaming these headstones, steles, chiselled urns,
Wreaths and leaves in low relief of sleep: Oh see,
Here is a red mirror of shining porphyry
In whose glow the eye observes itself observing

Itself, and on and on like that. Here is repose,
Figured in the stone pair lying above the ground,
Her knees raised and touching, he on his side by hers.
And here, worn down by the rages of wind and rain,
Two shapeless doggies keep faith with a broken slab.

And then, blocking the way of going on among
The memorials, seeming to face us from all
Corners from wherever we come toward it, that Face
Dangles from its snaky hairdo, cold, half-smiling
So that even close up its mouth waits in the near
Distance. No old, contorted visage of horror
We know from wisdom's shield regards us in this clear,
Gray afternoon light that calls the grassiest greens
Forth from themselves. It is another gaze, as from
Memorials of our own we once made, that now
Would petrify our eyes and turn our tongues to grass.
It is as if we made her in our images.

So that, fleeing back down the cold, light, roofless aisles
Where recall bounces back from unechoing stones,
We rerun mazes of our late meandering
Among these short, arresting inscriptions and this
Smarmy memorializing. We bump against
Knowing that it was not in pursuit of solid
Pictures that we wandered in among all this, but
That there need be no seeking that which sleeps away
In stone for which the living butterfly is but
An image, as of its own fluttering shadow;
That the tombstones were there wherever we were then,
Where we are now, wherever there is wandering.

Thus what we should have wanted all along—boxes
Of glass, showing through it the grass, other boxes,
And some of the sky from which the eye turns, flying
Its own unlikeness—now seem a last resort, not
To be found anymore. And here where space seems now
To be carved out of the bright stone that shadows it,

Perhaps a monument of eternal crystal
Might yet remain one with what it recollected,
And with reflections on and in it. It would be
More difficult to enter than one of those stone
Closed doorways cut into the sky, the grass. It would
Be empty of itself, and bright with what was meant.

Richard Howard

Stitching in Time: Dorothy Ruddick

The only god whose name
we know: Mutation . . .

Remember that day on the beach, remember
   how we marveled at the sea's design
     abandoned merely to chance—
unpredictable, inevitable, so
   we called it chance—that shining scarf of foam
     repeatedly wreathed on itself
in the long love-letters ocean writes to land?

Remember then the bonfire we found—burnt out,
   the ashes organized by their spent
     soul into the fire's design,
dying in whispers we were not meant to hear,
   till only the song was left, silent
     structure of the log that once
had shouted green as any limb in our woods?

And the clouds came on, faster it seemed for all
   the light they limited, until one
     kind of future was past: gone
in the altered pattern of a darkness asking
   no more than submission from the air—
     remember the clouds that afternoon,
racing each other to see which would fade first?

But earth faded first, remember? how the fields
   went out, or went up into darkness,
     clambering above themselves
like a clumsy burglar leaving too many
   clues to a far from perfect crime: night
     never falls, night rises, and this—
this after all can happen only on earth.

Water and fire, air and the ground, losing and

[75]

gaining at once—elements always
    simultaneously say
Yes and No—you have remembered! Here they are
    on the modest cloth, intricate
      obstinance of the insect
combining with the mystic's fixed ambition
    to declare, stitch by stitch, what cannot
      be abridged: *this has the ring's*
will in it, this joy, this renunciation
    of yourself, of whatever is not
      chosen. Between Arachne
who made too well and Penelope who unmade,
    you have gone about your daily task,
      the business of purgatory.
Ask the fact for the form: material things!

Richard Hugo

Last Words to James Wright

I'll call you Bedford, Ed. That's what you called me.
The plane lifts off the runway, circles left across
the mountains, straightens and heads east.
I'm reading in New York and Zetta's coming.
Ed was you, was me, our private ploy.
He lasted thirty years. Now one of Ed is gone.
And what's one Ed alone? You told me January 3
they'd operate in time and damn it, Jim,
I took that as a promise. I really did.
Ed Bedford, you bastard, you lied.

This time, the branch is broke. In early work
you urged the criminal, the derelict,
the dispossessed to run between the stars.
You wanted words to sing the suffering on
and every time you asked the words came willing.
I'm toasting you in heaven, four miles over Billings.
When I see Zetta, your wife,
I'll kiss her. I'll call her Annie for luck.
I'm scared as hell nothing's going to work.
Ed Bedford, you bastard, you lied.

You're the only man I knew outside of me
quoted Robert Benchley, same passages in fact.
You need every laugh you get
when your hometown's stocked with broken souls.
You left and couldn't leave that dirty river town
where every day the dirty river rolls.
I'll toast you on the Minneapolis layover.
As Rodney Dangerfield puts it, Ed:
"It's not easy, life. Not easy at all."
Make it Scotch and dirty river water.

Now the New York leg, nonstop. The midwest

moves back in the dark, now and then
the dull electric burn of town, the dark again.
Off left, some shining major city. Remember, Jim,
when they seemed glamourous, filled with magnificent women
you'd never find at home. That and the need to run,
the gift that sent a raw boy nonstop
over a green wall, over a green world,
star to star, buddy to dubious saints.
What poet ever found a synonym for shame.

Those saints in solitary where the dirty river rolls,
they know each life clicks off and on,
the off darker than a shabby habit,
the on more blinding than a stray star in the kitchen.
Jesus, Jim, the starker the fact I'm facing
the less I want to sing. Sorry, Ed,
to be so goddam serious. We've got your poems.
We've all got at least two names.
But which one gives and keeps his word?
Ed Bedford, you bastard, you lied.

Ed Bedford, you bastard, you died.
What a chill. We circle the Statue of Liberty.
I feel no liberty at all on the final approach.
I feel a little drunk and a lot more empty,
like passing through some unknown factory town
knowing it must be home.
Be glad of the green wall you climbed across one day.
Be glad as me.
I forgive you, Ed, even if I did swear never.
What's a lie between Eds? What's one more dirty river?

T. R. Hummer

The Second Story

And we may well heave a sigh of relief at the
thought that it is nevertheless vouchsafed to a few
to salvage without effort from the whirlpool of
their own feelings the deepest truths, towards which
the rest of us have to find our way through tor-
menting uncertainty and with restless groping.
—Freud

On the other side of the arc-light-level window
Hung at the top of that slope of Victorian porch,
Someone believes in the laying on of hands,

Or some two believe, and the woman of them sings
Her hymn. It comes down to me where I stand unashamed
To listen, unashamed to be here under these morning stars

Where they do not know I am, where no one should be.
This is the life in the body, certainty, uncertainty:
I am here, and if they knew they would not be

What I imagine so easily, the woman a darkness
In the shadow the man above her casts, starlight and arclight
From the window by the bed eclipsing his face from her,

Her legs lifted around him in that delicate poise
Of the almost-come, so when he lowers
His invisible mouth that could be any man's

And takes her breast, her knees stiffen in the same
Upward motion that suddenly and beautifully breaks
This contralto out of her as the freed light strikes

Her face: that, or some familiar variation. But if they knew
Another darkened body stood on the innocent
Corner of two sidewalks below them, listening,

What would they be? I ask myself and know:
Up there in that bedroom I can almost see
With its various reproductions—armoire, nightstand, vanity,

Surrounding its crucially refinished bed—
They would, if they could suddenly know me, stop
Their singular motion in the paralyzed reflex of fear,

Afraid, God help me, of nothing, of me,
A human stranger. So knowledge is fear.
I look up at the house spreading its white façade

Streetlight-struck in the blackness of this summer morning,
Five A.M., Vermont, windless and cloudless,
And I see, I want to tell myself simply,

A house, but I know it is no house
I ever lived in. These are the second homes
Of the rich, on a street of stained glass and cupolas

And high balconies where a clichéd lover might declaim
Wherefore? and the answer rise *What light?*
And where lawns of tame maples yield

That storied Vermont sweetness: sap.
I have come here insomniac, waked by a dream
Not frightening but strange in its inexplicable

And boring complications, the way the mind is,
And I remember the old joke: *The rich*
Are not like us, it goes, to which the answer is

The only one possible: *Right, they have more*
Money. I imagine those two up there, after,
Smoking identical Turkish cigarettes while he tells her

The details of an obscure incident from his childhood.
She nods in the dark and explains. After all,
Her Ph.D. is Viennese and psychological

And ought to do her some good in what she likes
To call her *private life*.
Yes, it is good to lie in the dark and breathe

That alien smoke through bruised lips, good to imagine
The love lives of distant and exotic peoples
In inner-city Detroit or Mississippi

And how, unexamined and mentally unhealthy,
They must hurt each other. And yes, it is good
To stand on the sidewalk hearing it go on and on,

That utterly unknowable woman transcendentally moaning
Out of a life I can only pretend to imagine,
And which I tell myself I could cause

To come to a crashing *coitus interruptus* by a single
Shouted word. Any word would do: *me*
I could yell, or *here*, or *Detroit*, or *dysfunction*,

It would all be the same word: *fear*.
So words are fear, as long as they let us know
Someone is out there, someone is close by, present

And mysterious in a body that has a familiar shape
But no known face. This is the life
In the body, what we know of each other, the nothing

Names tell us: this is the song
Of the woman touched by the man she thinks
She knows or loves or her life

Would be nothing without
Touching in rooms so dark nobody can say
Who anybody really is, where nobody has

Words songlike enough to touch
The reason I am out here, afraid
Of whoever is up there, lifted

In their Victorian construct
Over the world they speak to without knowing,
Moaning down their wordless and irrefutable explanations,

Giving hands and tongue to name me
Their human groping, making
What even the most petrified among us certainly

Could agree to call *love*, could say
Is good. But now her low voice rises
Toward a classic soprano. I feel its pure

Shudder low in my spine as she tells me
What I translate roughly as *My God
Someone is doing something right:*

And I know I have missed my chance, they are beyond me,
Too far gone for any word
I could shout ever to bring them down.

This is the rapture, these are the sinless
Raised beyond the reach of any voice
Of mine. This is salvation, I am forgiven

My fear and my dreams: I am foretold,
In this flesh that holds me, wherefore
What light (it is the east) grows suddenly unashamed

On the other side of trees that are only
Eclipses of themselves, thrown hard on the edge
Of this world's unearnable laying on of richness.

Richard Jackson

Greenwood

What I wanted to say to her
was the prayer the deer turn into
as they step deeper towards those woods
grazing on darkness, or the silence that is
the thistle light of their eyes staring back,
for whatever we say means something more.
In whatever language this was before
it was the snap of greenwood on coals
there is a word I have never spoken
that calls out to the hurt it belongs to
the way a flock of swallows, at dusk,
makes visible a turn of wind
and the night unhinges on that simple gesture.
Or her touch, say, across a table,
a woman so beautiful the deer abandon
whatever words I have invented for them
and turn to graze in a meadow or marsh
for herbs, salt grass, greenwood,
sometimes springing suddenly, whistling,
as they will, in a language of fear or surprise.

Pamela Kircher

The Intimate Earth

The Chinese know the space inside us
where the intimate earth of the eye
is painted as delicately as silk.
A land of mist,
pines twisted from years of wind.
Rocks cling to the moss that covers them
and pilgrims go far into the mountains to dwell in caves.
All this empties itself in grief,
gives up the tiny planes of a wasp's wing,
moist soil, apricot blossoms,
and the last curl of a wave.
The broken woman rises from sleep,
looks out her window,
and has no name for anything.

Judith Kitchen

Perennials

As if the mind could choose
what to recall. As if summer spread
at the back of the brain,
yellow petals drifting down
from the garage wall. One scent
and your bodies were hard
on the grass. Touch me, he said,
and you did, though
that is not really the story.

As if the body could be more
than a set of patterns.
More than a child who needs permission.
As if it asked for what
it will remember.

In Rio, in January, the sun
hammers all day at the lampposts.
Children rap all night
on the windows, asking for money.
They will not go away.
Nothing will ever go away.
Not the night with its cheap perfume,
not the arsenic glare on the rooftops.

White flower, white flower, yellow—
they push up through the ground
uncalled for. Planted
by someone else, another eye
determining their order.
I accept them the way I accept
what is not offered.

*

Touch me, you said, and I did.

The gardenia lasts twenty-five years and still
it is Easter morning.
And there's one white carnation
for the day we were married.
Yellow flowers, carelessly cut
and pasted, tumble from envelopes, wilt
on dashboards. Nameless daffodils, forsythia
spitting back the sun.
Why do I need to make sense of it?

William Kloefkorn

Taking the Milk to Grandmother

Not the milk, but the color of milk:
first snow unblemished in a bottle.
Not the bottle, but the feel of bottle
hard and cool against the curling
of a small boy's hand.

On the way, the bottle cradled
in my left arm,
I stop to watch old man Thornton's minks
rising on their hind legs in their cages
watching me.

Not the mink, but the smell of mink,
small manure that trails me down the alley
until, dissembled and sweet,
it becomes the girl the big boys in the bathroom
unzip themselves and over arcs of urine

talk about: Virginia Mae, downright pretty
if she'd lose a little weight,
who eats like a horse and screws like a mink—
not sex, but the heft of sex,
the motion and the smell of sex,

old man Thornton's minks in darkness
repeating themselves, the draw I descend
to begin that final leg to grandmother's house
downhill repeating itself, to the tracks and beyond,
footsteps, my own, repeating and repeating themselves,

until they carry me onto the back porch
where the screen door opens
and grandmother wide as a monument

fills the space and in both hands takes the milk
and invites me in for an oatmeal cookie

and the last of the milk from yesterday's bottle,
which rinsing and drying (her apron as towel,
the bluebells on her apron as towel:
not the bluebell, but the damp of bluebell
in the gnarl of hand that is grandmother)

she gives to me, bending gives to me,
with it a kiss that is the breath
of milk and cheese, the ancient aftermath of sex.
Kiss. Kiss. Kiss is the sound the act makes,
sex the mink that with its small manure

defines Virginia Mae. Halfway home
I toss the bottle into the air end over end.
At the end of the alley the milkcow grazes:
not the cow, but the ripening of cow,
day into day the ripening of udder

into the ripening of tit,
milk then into the pail and into the bottle
that hard and cool against the curling
of a small boy's hand
finds its way into the hands of grandmother.

Tit. Not tit, but the sound of tit,
an empty bottle that having descended
end over end
from the height of its grand ascension
strikes the hand.

Ted Kooser

Just Now

Just now, if I look back down
the cool street of the past, I can see
streetlamps, one for each year,
lighting small circles of time
into which someone will step
if I squint, if I try hard enough—
circles smaller and smaller,
leading back to the one faint point
at the start, like a star.
So many of them are empty now,
those circles of roadside and grass.
In one, the moth of some feeling
still flutters, unspoken,
the cold darkness around it enormous.

Maxine Kumin

Orb

Having been raised in the fine mimetic
Tradition of poetic moons, O moon,
Makes you no more or less poetic
Though me more wary, shunning June
And all allusions to Diana, bows,
Arrows, love, love's lunacy,
Hot velvet nights, soft does
Or eyes as shy as.
            Orb of my quandary,
Bard bayed at, runic maniacal
Tide-tugger, seed-sower;
Sulfurous languorous zodiacal
Monocled eye, O glower!

Greg Kuzma

The Great Poems

The great poems, surely they
are without people in them. For when people intrude
there are dishes, there is the smell of people,
there are arms and eyes,
there is the brain having let the body slip.
But in the great poems there is only a flower or two,
and the wind playing leapfrog with itself. Perhaps
you do not understand or agree, but in the great poems
man arrives too late for the action, the accident
having occurred—he puts out his feeble hands, and
the blood is immense like the sea, or the bones
cannot be mended, or, dropped on its stem, the head
of the flower is down and its color gone. Lament
the loss. This is what the great poems do.
The bird which just now fled beyond your reach
or thought. The stone which the stream washes over and
over. Each day the sun creeps close over the earth
to free its colors.

Sydney Lea

Horn

You always named it
the long way for some reason:
shell of a conch,
syllables that scanned
like *son of a bitch,*
though it was only
as angry as you
ever got. Not very. No,
Father: sad. Sad, then still;
and I can't tell you how
much sadder-sounding now.

You blew, it mourned
something, it wound
through secret paths
that I and my brothers—all
living then—had made
like qualifications
in the syntax of a man
reluctantly becoming
a realist. It knew
no abbreviation,
but tongued each
leaf, each stone
as it cozened us home.

We could come home slow though,
for it wasn't the porch bell's
paratactic clamor,
expletive of terror:
Death! Drowning! Fire!
All rare
in recollection, though each
has been spoken for later.

An apparently casual
call, unchildlike, summons
to bed or meal, incidentals
in a lengthy period. We ambled,
therefore, pausing
to imagine fatal
copperheads on ledges, staring
at the high ridge
with its flecked aura
of buzzards, nudging
a great toad, trying out
new risky words . . .

Let me render the sound. I can.
It held even then
the pain we feel
when we must
turn to what we have
no choice but to turn to.
Resignation's
utterance, born into us,
inflection alone
remaining to be
recalled and apprehended. Not
the percussive of lust,
or catastrophe, not
the quick announcement,
midnight
phone call, bowel-shivering news
of a lover's unfaith, not
the heart-freezing
instant of diagnosis
but protracted
unease for which
the diagram is there
from the start, and on which
we gradually heap
our meanings, as flesh avails
itself of the articulate frame. Not

the hiss of the snake,
then, but as if
—in the ear's eccentric funnels—
his sound were the echo
of his body's shape,
near-comatose on the bone-
warming rocks of noon.
Or the buzzard's orotund
glidings spelled
lethargic long vowels:
"Come HOME, Come HOME..."
Or the toad's pace
determined the meter
of our steps
homeward to the low
windings of the shell.

Not, therefore, shock
but circumlocution
of somberer fear:
slow homing,
meandering and glissando
of the conch's husk
the muddled signals of young
nemesis borne into later life
and named: vagueness,
collapse of margins, clarity
absent as night
comes on.

As night came on that night
when you beckoned
over and over,
but each time it seemed
from a different quarter,
as if you had entered the shadow-
flesh of the night-
jar whose call
imprecisely parses woods

and meadows, so is a dream
that shifts just
as you reach its stop.
Some knowledge
it may have been that stopped you
from clattering the bell.
The reluctance of summer
light in its dying? Awareness
of what we would later
plead? "We were trying . . ."
Easy sentence, come to be juxtaposed
now, as I put the horn
to my lips, blow
into it forty angry years,
and all they've cost: obscenity,
imperative, then the wailed
feckless interrogative
summons. And still,
you are lost.

Philip Levine

Any Night

Look, the eucalyptus, the atlas pine,
the yellowing ash, all the trees
are gone, and I was older than
all of them. I am older than the moon,
than the stars that fill my plate,
than the unseen planets that huddle
together here at the end of a year
no one wanted. A year more than a year,
in which the sparrows learned
to fly backwards into eternity.
Their brothers and sisters saw this
and refuse to build nests. Before
the week is over they will all
have gone, and the chorus of love
that filled my yard and spilled
into my kitchen each evening
will be gone. I will have to learn
to sing in the voices of pure joy
and pure pain. I will have to forget
my name, my childhood, the years
under the cold dominion of the clock
so that this voice, torn and cracked,
can reach the low hills that shielded
the orange trees once. I will stand
on the back porch as the cold
drifts in, and sing, not for joy,
not for love, not even to be heard.
I will sing so that the darkness
can take hold and whatever
is left, the fallen fruit, the last
leaf, the puzzled squirrel, the child
far from home, lost, will believe
this could be any night. That boy,
walking alone, thinking of nothing

or reciting his favorite names
to the moon and stars, let him
find the home he left this morning,
let him hear a prayer out
of the raging mouth of the wind.
Let him repeat that prayer,
the prayer that night follows day,
that life follows death, that in time
we find our lives. Don't let him see
all that has gone. Let him love
the darkness. Look, he's running
and singing too. He could be happy.

Last Song of the Angel of Bad Luck

What chance do I have? No one
would bend to hear my lament,
no one would think I suffer.
Like a chemical, I carry a map
that takes me always to you
and to you, who despise me.
I'm going away, into the cities
you have burned or blighted
or the valleys of abandoned farms.
I will suffer privation, the sun,
the cold, loneliness, whatever
the world is and is not
without me, so that I may
come back human or animal,
something without wings
or conscience, so that I may
have a chance, a small chance.

Who

Why am I going away from the glass of wine
from the loaf of bread
Why am I not mourning the tiny death
of the sparrow
who leaped on the lowest branches
of the atlas pine
until one afternoon he was drawn
into tall burning grass
What will I say when the nights grow
longer and longer
the dawn is barely visible, a grudging
of yellow light
The day dies into the violet halos
of exhaust
No one takes my hand and leads me to bed
to the ceremony of breath
the mouth to mouth agonies of darkness
we grew to live
How will I know I was and I was alive
when this passes
Who will take my hand and lead me to you
to my beloved
the man I always was, the woman I became
the one body and the other
Who will take my hand that is on fire
that smells of earth
that is burning now to an autumnal rust
and is all I need
Who will lead me to the ceremonies of sorrow
who will lead me

Susan Ludvigson

Lesson

My father said quicksand
might be hidden in the tall swamp-grass,
would suck me down, down
to the center of the earth.
Even in fall, the dry season,
when the horses snapped reeds
with each step,
a fearful swarm of insects
could mean that pit,
wet as fresh manure, was only disguised,
leaves covering it over like a blind.
Mother, no Ceres, did not believe
I would disappear. Watch
for blackbirds, she said,
handing me the old wicker basket.
Wherever they land is safe.
Bring me the small blue flowers
that grow close to the ground
and the tallest cattails
you can find.
I followed those redwings in
feeling like Gretel, whistling for courage.
When I came out,
a mass of cattails over my shoulder
like a bag of gold,
basket filled with blossoms,
she was waiting at the edge,
waving and smiling.

I Arrive in a Small Boat, Alone

In my bed your body is an island
inhabited by a cautious race of men
whose elaborate rituals were designed
for safety, like the shaking of hands
to show an absence of weapons,
or the sharing of food to prove its purity.
They are united, they rally
to a common cause, so that
when possible danger appears,
they line up, each with one knee
on the ground for balance,
shields side by side,
the reflected sun bright enough
to blind the approaching figure,
me, waving a hand.
Now and then one's caught by himself
off-duty, the tribe's chant
dim in the distance. Sometimes
he hears a song that seems
to come from his own blood's rhythm.
But he checks himself,
returns to the village quickly,
rarely tripping on roots,
for he's memorized the path,
cut away offending branches.
Safely back, he joins the others,
sleeps in his own hut, in tune
with the breath of his brothers.
He knows if he keeps still long enough
the music will stop.

Dexter Masters

Graffiti for a Particle Accelerator

We have suffered enough to be wise.
Why we're not we can only surmise.
Perhaps in the end
We prefer to pretend
That the whats tell us more than the whys.

We have suffered enough. To be wise
Is no doubt the remaining surprise.
But the primary task
Is to know what to ask,
And who's to decode the replies?

We have suffered! Enough! To be wise
We will have to start using our eyes!
No more contravening
Of words and their meaning—
Let's scrutinize! crystallize! cut to size!

Have we suffered enough to be wise?
Can we see what's behind the disguise?
If we find out what's there
(And when it is where)
Will the truth tell us more than the lies?

Sumio Matsuda

Views of an American Writer

When he recalled the past
always
he remembered the way the weather was,

how people
in their prime years
were swept by a cold wind
from northern mountains,
altered by the snow of high countries,
changed by small rains
or hard ones,
with always a steady sun
presiding over flesh;

how ideas eroded
eventually
like the soft hills
of yet another marvelous country;

but in the meanwhile
how they ate
and drank wine
in the lovely cities
of their weather's time;

and always
how our bones lay
inches away
from the immortality
of pine-tree forests
and deep ocean currents.

Jack Matthews

The People in These Houses

I'm not depressed, as I walk along this street,
by the age of these old houses; it's not the weight
of years that bothers me. The only vestiges
inside these walls are of a material state:
wicker chairs, arthritic from thirty winters,
a sofa mildewed by the basement weather,
and boxes filled with letters not worth saving.
I don't believe that here, in this stale climate,
ghosts live on to curse the merely living.
I fear another kind of curse that works inside,
worse than imagined sin behind closed shutters,
that the people here are still more deeply haunted
by nothing, nothing in their hearts to hide.

William Matthews

Flood

Strange to think what solvents
we carry to work and back,
or even on the dull miracles
of commercial flight, and through
O'Hare among the composed
blank faces of the all-day
travelers not squandering
their attentions here, where
there's so little to love and all
of it scratched and marred,
like the faces we love because they
are not strange. And strange to think,
as Braniff launches one of its blue
boomerangs to Dallas and back,
how seldom we use some
of those solvents but carry them
anywhere, like an army, in case,
in case. . . . Should one of us need
suddenly to weep, he might start
(if he wept seldom) like a car
on a cold morning, but soon
weeping is its own event
and the body like a rented hall,
and all too soon the party's
over. I better clean this mess,
he thinks. It's like defrosting
the old fridge from boyhood,
all the blurred fur of ice
turns cloudy water, gets thrown
away. The details pool and then
they're not details, they're
experience. Gone is the sound
of a fireplace one day: the seethe
of green wood first and then

suddenly the flames flapping
like hot cloth. Gone is the smell
of that one overripe Pont L'Eveque: hay
steeped in cow urine. And gone
is the speed of the barn settling
around him as a child, and the
blue dark before dawn, the thick
shifting cows, the itch of a new
flannel shirt, and the delirium
of being up among huge, warm
shapes when he should be asleep.
But it's gone, along with the path
to get to or from it, along with how
to remember between times
the exact pressure of her head
on his shoulder; it's been washed
away and that's why he wept
who feels lightened now,
though someone else is weeping
near Gate E5, and the other
solvents—it's almost that we serve
them, we who are not anonymous—
we bear on our inexplicable
missions slosh gently inside
us, ready when we are.

Mekeel McBride

Once Upon a Time

It was winter. The woman wearing scarves of rain
made a mouth on the stream's skin
by throwing in her wedding ring. The mouth
widened into a wail that looped snakelike
into a spiny tree and watched you
with eyes unblinking as emeralds.

She gives you bouquets of bone-white lilies
with your name printed like a kiss on each puffy lip.
She slips away. She falls asleep for a hundred years
and dreams of swallowing roses soft as your tongue.
Find her, free her from this spell
that tells her she will never grow old. You try
to buy her heart with an apple that will not bruise.
But when you find her she has fallen in love
with the woodcutter the evil brother. They claim her
by the bloodied axe, the apple broken open as if
it were your body. Behind you, they fill your footprints
with fresh earth to keep you from ever going back.

Martha McFerren

Mountain Soprano

1.

She sits on a pattern called Temperance Tree.
I've forgotten her name. She looks like me
captured in British bone and skin.
If I turn the daguerreotype in my hand
she's not my mother, but only light,
an amber mirror that shows my face.
Both of us dabbled in second sight,
held in the blindness of breed and place.

Another century called the tune,
the lyrics drawn from a great reserve:
lady anonymous left alone
beneath the arc of a willow curved
to such perfection it isn't real,
but tinted in oleograph genteel
or done at school by a preacher's daughter
whose world was tempera thinned with water.
But the woman is real; her weight of skirt
cuts a scar in the new world dirt
and she waits forever, her folded hands
beyond admission, beyond demands.

Once, relying on things not seen,
she stood at a mirror combing her hair—
that's an old, old conjure for Halloween.
She lifted an apple, but as she stared
against the glass with her lack of sight
no future Adam appeared for a bite.
No lowlands rider stood over her shoulder;
she saw herself, but a legend older
with eyes two leaflets of shallow mint
and hair in gathers, an auburn shawl.
And this is the way it always went.

*

She gave up witching that very fall
and made a bargain: a foursquare bed.
Don't do it, honey, her granny said.
But she was finished with spinster moons
and games of choosing. She got a lover
plus china cups and a dozen spoons
and a fine assortment of Briarknot covers.
This was the only working pact.

She learned to cherish what she could have,
be decently wary of what she lacked
and credit the healing of Gilead.
And though Belial was kept at bay,
the water and bacon kept somewhat pure,
most of her children were weed and clay.
A few ceased quickly, and some endured
a brace of winters before they died
to lie unstained with a token spray
while all the viable kinfolk cried.

With no alternative but to pray
she met each cross in her better dress,
admonished to love, obliged to bury.
The grim but requisite waxy kiss.
Her own particular death to carry,
though it was less an astonishment
for half her nation was dying young,
each, again, with a mute consent
and the limited choice of womb or lung:
the precious damage of motherhood
or the virgin hemorrhage in the throat.

None of the doctors was any good.
She kept the evenings to sew and wait,
ripping her dresses for counterpanes:
ugly homespun or fine delaine
all more durable than herself,
a woman finished and neatly shelved
at thirty-eight to discreetly fade

and be replaced from the ambuscade
of fresh young daughters. The work remained:
the cornbread, basting, and soap to set,
and also the remnants that granny sang
and nobody's daughter could quite forget—
each subversion a woman's own,
though purged of the usual slight revenge
and never sung when her man was home.
She kept her center until the end.

And this is the way it always went:
three graves to the grave of the patriarch,
the last of England twisted and spent.
But in the interim no one marked
the music channeling in our heads.
Not everything over the water is dead.
If you sing for long, it becomes the truth,
the gramarye broken and almost gone:
condemned as heathen, of no good use,
but still suspiciously full of charms—
fragments of riddle and nursery rhyme,
the incongruities soothed by time
and spiked with fennel and local guns.

I know myself how a dulcimer thrums,
a subtle instrument honed so fine
the music within it could spill like wine
if wine were allowed. It lays a trap,
the pliant hourglass in our laps
reckoning time as a raw response:
the wisp of rhythm that always stays
and wills us into experience.
I've heard you have to be lonesome to play,
though I've never figured whom that excludes.

During one of my stranger moods
I learned the ballad of Sarah Moss
whose sweetheart came as he'd promised her
after her daddy had run him off

for no real reason. People swear
one night he tapped on her windowpane
and rode her off on a deadened mare.
All she felt was a heavy rain.
Ahead, at a juncture of grass and air,
the lightning crafted a heavy scrawl:
within each crevice the beasties crawled
from Revelation without a sound.
Every lodging was fallen down,
every lantern peculiar haze.

She thought they were gone for seven days
but then in silence he set her down
on a bit of remarkably normal ground
and Sarah finally understood
her only honest escape was dead—
a week in Frankfort, and she no more
than a mile or two from her father's door.
They hadn't actually gotten away.

And that was when she learned to play,
using a feather to work her songs
into a unit made double strong:
rags of prophecy, fire and hunger,
all herself—grown a legend younger,
and rocking through passions and gallows trees
with a dulcimer angled across her knees.

2.

At certain seasons on mountain time
an irregular music begins to climb
and hold the country for miles around:
a pure and coldly relentless sound,
full of knowing. Distorted, it swells.
With keen ingratitude women rise
from darker passages no one tells
and watch the hills with ignited eyes.

*

The women are singing, their presence sure,
a coming judgment on broken ground.
In spite of heaven they persevered,
their pretty images left behind,
buried dolls in a night of grass:
the waxen baby, the wooden chit,
the Frozen Charlotte, its hands shut fast
and lips compressed in a china pout
like when its namesake defied the snow
and whispered, I'm growing warmer now,
but never grew warmer. Every doll
a penny of century molded true—
truer, perhaps, than a living child.

Bisque and papier-mâché endure
but every owner is flesh and dead.
Papa resurrected the dolls instead—
papas do that when they have a choice.
A rag doll sobs in a cotton voice
so childish that mockingbirds pause and stare
between each tug at its raveled hair.
And there was another mockingbird
that dipped its bill in a woman's blood
and sang her murderer's name at home
(tell the world that I died for love)
and the boy broke down and confessed his crime.

There was a girl up in a pine
who saw her lover one night alone
digging a grave for a pretty corpse.
She knew the next was her very own
so at their wedding she told her folks:
I was high and he was low,
the cock did cry and the wind did blow.
The tree did shake and my heart did ache
to see what a hole the Fox would make.
And they guessed her riddle and shot him dead.

*

(Don't do it, honey, her granny said.
Don't go at all. If you go, you'll die.)
Nobody knows where the dangers lie
and often it seems the only ones
who truly survived that western run
were the breathing puppets, arranged in place,
their hands subdued and their perfect faces
void of passion. The rest are gone.

Even the brown girl, herself betrayed
to a stiff Jacobean bridal gown,
was a helpless Eve in a mystery play
without the artifice she would need
to slow the passion of plow and seed.
Powdered in time to a makeshift pale,
she knelt to death in a farthingale
on flagstones mortared in British ice.
The sweet, unreadable sacrifice
beyond evasion: Rebecca, at last,
harmonized to another past,
her altered rhythms and altered eyes
laid away by the younger son
in the older version of paradise.

Like the country, the night moves on.
Close to midnight a woman stands
waiting for travelers on the road,
a spray of lilac in her hand.
A fancy gig or a wagonload
of backwoods cotton is no concern,
as long as it's moving. Her features burn
like Baldwin's light on a single pine—
a curious, phosphorescent shine.
Lady anonymous on the prowl,
going discreetly from hill to town
armed with a sharpened edge of smile.

Father is nothing and mother is worn
and full of bitterness for her life.

She wielded her child like a silver knife
to hamstring masters and make them crawl.
One man's excuse for consuming all,
another's reason for burning out,
she squanders demurely, her smile devout
and calm as a Charleston boarding school.
A camisoled angel knows every rule:
eradicate filthiness and affection.
Arsenic gives her a saint's complexion,
luxury teaches her how to freeze.
In villages haunted by riven trees,
in drab mill towns, on eroded farms,
the constant lie in each other's arms,
clawing and yielding and falling still.
A woman stands on a lilac hill
smiling and breathing a virgin scent;
her face is porcelain set with flint.

Beyond the reach of a meetinghouse spire
the night expands to a final fire
with faces wavering in the throe:
laughing faces. Beneath its bow
a senile fiddle begins to whine
in a mountain soprano like turpentine:
a black-haired man in a frosty bracken
playing The Devil's Dream as fact.
A scarecrow flinches. It knows the tune.

Dance on the riverbank, follow the moon,
combining hands in a serpentine
as wild as a hound in a nameless thorn,
as ruffled as *Godey's Magazine*.
The fiddler dominates every turn
and reel, contriving a metered feast
of careless killings, disturbing beasts
and ruined towers within his call.
Did he cry there was no more west at all?

*

Forget your color is gone so pale,
forget the blood in the icy well
and dance on a shingle of crusted mud.
The music is cinnamon in your blood,
redder than oxygen. Keep the pace:
your hair is a curtain blown over your face
shutting out manners and morning dew.
You dance alone, nothing touches you,
a solitary with Calvin's brand,
escaped from a Protestant caravan
and bound for the country of true release.

The fiddler's hands are sinew and musk.
Playing a game of cat and mouse,
he strips a red ear out of its husk
and dangles it over your nose and smiles.
You stare at his mouth like a cornered child.
Within a second the air is warm:
a day of children's possessive arms,
the old apostles, the fresh green mound.
And you realize that your hands are bound.

Tamer, more diffident than before,
the music lingers a stanza more
then parts in fragments along a ridge.
A single timber becomes a bridge
across a river of chilling foam.
The man in penumbra sees Nellie home.

3.

She left the coverlet on her bed
with no allowance for disarray,
every parcel and crimson thread
evaluated. And there it lay:
square as a ballad, precisely sung
and bramble-stitched by a needle tongue.
Today my sentient fingers trace
all Appalachia across its face,
the merge of fabrics as good as new:

gray raccoons in their private snow,
a dozen ponies with tendril manes
set in a valley of narrow grass,
lovers who conquer and part again,
all the world and a looking glass.

A Yankee peddler opens his pack.
Tell me, ladies, what do you lack?
Licorice drops or watered scents,
bundles of fanciful compliments,
horehound, buttons, or Paisley shawls?
All the world is a crimson skein,
all the world a pomander ball.
Under a feather of summer rain
a girl set loose at a country fair
holds a black ribbon against her hair
and pays the price with a secret kiss.
All the world is a clasp of stones,
bits of carnelian or amethyst
strung in rows on a golden chain.

A witch girl tosses a mass of seeds,
fertile dice in her grimy hand:
hellebore, sassafras, fever tree,
cohosh root and sweet marjoram,
and goldenseal with its juicy core.
They say bitumen makes open sores,
pellagra spreads like a butterfly
across your skin. They say that knot
is a wreath of canker, that milky eye
is from the ancients who've always sat
with white, blind fishes down in the caves,
even before the Indians came.

They say blind nettle will quicken love.
Elderberry turns wild dogs tame.
A wooden nickel will buy the wind
and a sweetbriar thicket will hold it penned.
Riddle my riddle, answer right,

where was I last Saturday night?
Queen Anne, Queen Anne sits in the sun:
if you can't love all, then you must love one,
if you can't love one, then you must love all.
The lady unravels her knitting ball,
the lady dissolves. In a shuttered room
she weaves herself on an awkward loom,
its warp composed of a flock of knives,
its weft of music. The draft survived
from another country. In smoky light,
with a thousand stitches, insanely tight,
the kingdom comes on a square of cloth
to trim a parsonage. Soft as a moth,
devoid of color, she threads away.

A conscious article on display,
she crochets yardage of pillow trim
and filigree waste for a pretty hem.
The thread was spun on the Natchez Trace;
a woman sits with her ropes of lace
under a burden of heavy hair
(the hunter married the silver knife).
She nods and sinks in her wicker chair,
lady anonymous as a wife
embroidering charity day by day.
Somebody folded the west away
and the colors faded. The best men won.
Queen Anne, Queen Anne sits in the sun.

One long winter there was a child
who stood each day at the windowpane
holding a brown-eyed china doll,
and her mother inscribed with a diamond ring
Ellen stood here to watch the snow
on the square of glass and added the year.
All such a long, long time ago
but the glass remains. The doll is here,
propped on the coverlet of my bed.
A quilt so heavy it sleeps like lead:

too heavy to lay on the crushed desire
of my child, well-fed behind barbed wire
and caught as myself. If I could sing
as my mother did, I'd sing you this
with the Anglo-Saxon quaver and sting
bred in my fiber. I'd sing of force
that comes from anger. I'd sing of art
that passed as labor to stay alive
and tell how mountains were gouged apart,
my tension requisite to describe
the lack of tension before each kill.

I came this way of my own free will
as far as it reaches, which isn't far.
I crossed a sea in the past, I know,
where Papist devils worried the spars.
I built an instrument of my own
and made up Scripture and Turkey-Tracks.
I knew a woman whose hair stayed black
for seven decades. There was a fall
and cane stalks broken and slowly boiled
to a saccharine lava. There was a cat.
But the renovation of damaged patterns
makes no sense for the daughter I bred.
She moves to a music I never made,
straight and blind as a Buddhist arrow.

I think there's quicksilver in her marrow.
She doesn't sleep easily. During the night
she often rises and stays for hours
by a hawthorn, watching the migrant lights
and groping for suns like a carnal flower.
Beyond all reason, she strains like a child
for the arms of the air. She's cold and wild
yet I think she's going where she belongs:
into an absence. But I remain,
an anachronism forever drawn
between the pain and the lack of pain.
I am transition, a foxfire thread

that closes each faction and binds each break
and winds on a spindle dark as blood
with a rhythm as severed as Franklin's snake.
Both rattle supinely: Unite or Die.
Always the music is incomplete
yet promising gardens of rich device.
Like my nation, I always cheat,
I'm never what I was supposed to be.
Lift me up, song: this once, I'm free.

Peter Meinke

50 on 50

On my 50th birthday I shall give up symbols:
no more pools or tunnels, it's flat statements
from now on. What good is being 50
if you can't loosen your belt and be disgusting?
The world is blessed by beautiful women,
I will cry. *Which is not lovely at 9 p.m.?*
A fair number, perhaps, but just look at the men
slouching toward Florida with crooked teeth!
I have been embarrassed so often by now
I've developed a hump, but
can I look into her eyes and say,
You are average, my dear, only average?
And yet, that's what I love so much,
my heart faints before imperfections,
the sag, wrinkle, distracting blemish:
we are not mannikins, after all.
You have known love and been used hard,
I will say; you were taken to movies
and fuzzy hands groped at your nervous knees.
On public beaches randy twits nuzzled your breasts
while your eyes rolled wildly between ointments.
Maybe this is love, you thought, too generous as usual.
Women have always been generous, even the clothes
you wear a free gift to man
who should kneel down in his baggy pants
and flowered shirt to offer praise. I
will order coffee and sit in supermarkets
all day watching you wheel through
in your shorts and halters, adorable sad faces
twisted in concentration, torn between
canned peaches and pineapple chunks, the store-brand
detergent or the trusted Dash. And meat!
How you bend over the counter, hair in your eyes,
puzzling the bloody packages, fatty

content and artificial coloring.
O you should charge a fee for the back of your knees!
I see stories in each line, in each vein
running its startling course. Your son was an angel,
he sells typewriters now, and when you carried
him in your arms his small hands tugged at your
chin and lips, learning the feel of women.
And your daughter, really, looks just like you,
you can see it in the eyes, she tells you
everything when she comes home to visit:
Men are such children, they are not bad exactly
but sort of warped or frozen like an old movie
at the wrong speed. For my next 50 years
I want to study woman until I open
like a child's hand, like a mother's eye,
like you, love, in your patchwork corner.

James Merrill

Page from the Koran

A small vellum environment
Overrun with black
Scorpions of Kufic script—their ranks
All trigger tail and gold vowel-sac—
At auction this mild winter morning went
For six hundred Swiss francs.

By noon, fire from the same blue heavens
Had half erased Beirut.
Allah be praised, it said on crude handbills,
For guns and Nazarenes to shoot.
"How gladly with proper words," said Wallace Stevens,
"The soldier dies." Or kills.

God's very word, then, stung the heart
To greed and rancor? Yet
Not where its last glow touches one spare man
Inked-in against his minaret
—Letters so handled they are life, and hurt,
Leaving the scribe immune.

W. S. Merwin

Stairs

Long spiraling
descent by night
to the end of the last
metal
and the mind in the glass crown
that stole the mother's
daughter
down many steps I carry
the mirror my own size
into the dark
carrying it as a door a wing
an ear a skin
like my own
and if I fall every piece of us both
will reflect part of the floor
or ceiling of the palace stair
the waters of the earth
will drip into the pieces backwards
and flow on inventing forgetting
melting the pieces away to be born elsewhere
all on the same day early in the morning
leaves in dew before birds sing
or relics in the crystal treasure
but if I arrive without falling
this time

Fate

Cloud in the morning
evening a white opal
after a white sun
the lighted opal sits on the rim
of dark mountains
some are born hearing dogs bark in the mountains
among high walls just after sunset
and all their lives things are known to them
that are not known even to those born hearing water
or trees or sobbing or flutes or laughing

Jane Miller

The Stagger of the Wind
That I Think Is Your Turning

It's startling when a dog enters
the cold summer water,
and bullfrogs too, who are part
of the language, are part of the world
we drift through to remember.
We are and trail like adults
who visit their family graves, deaf
to each other while inwardly
mouthing: *one squirrel, two day lilies, three saints.*

The spiral is natural. In Dubuffet's garden of surface,
black and white lines run like stories
that never wear shoes,
knowingly choosing
the wooded way home.
It's only a story we trust
to ourselves: how love starts us
thinking in color again, while perfectly still,
moves up the strings of the sun rays

grazing the rose-weeds and limbs. It is,
it is like that: one day in the park you feel
proof like the hard flesh of apples
come falling. A last match is struck
and when hands take it further in,
we see ourselves in relation, smoke
the sun reddens, eyes
down, feeling the wind break
our grip.

Scott Minar

Luminare

Old glass has waves and shares the bending
of light with rain
and a still pond.
Such are my windows:
a man and woman walking
in the street
pulse laterally,
shifting as if the day
could no longer hold them.
We walked past sumac saplings
through crabgrass standing
at strange angles to the pocked
hillside, down
into the railroad tunnel,
the darkest plane in the world.
There, in the arches cut
into the wall, we
found the last refuge
of danger.
When our skin touched,
the sickly sweet taste of salt
and flesh was so new
and remembered
that the pain outside
was gone.
We whispered to each other
in the dark,
as the cattails whispered
waving between the cracked and broken
rules: the ties
oozing tar in the heat outside a tunnel
that had no color at all

by its nature.
But it glistens nonetheless,
like nothing else
in this world.

Judson Mitcham

Where We Are

Coals raked out on hearthstones writhe like men.
Lake weeds resemble a madonna, and great rocks
erode into profiles, smiling at clown-faced clouds
or frowning, puzzled as they peer far down
at long-dry stream beds, unable to find old light.
Blossom, starfish, mandrake, shadows in snow
open their arms. Everywhere, eyes spiral:
in the leaves of waterlilies they are amazed,
in slow creeks' vortices sleepy, a little sad,
in wood grain knowing, nearly sensual, in wings
of hawkmoths, blind. And hands are found in coral,
ears in shells, the small breasts of young girls
in tree trunks, skulls in walnuts. But faces
draw us as though we were infants to chrysalids
swaying on the underside of leaves, to sawn marble
and photos of the surface of Mars, to ice melting
an old man into the wind, to hollow, dead trees
and shacks blank-eyed on hills. There is also Christ
burned into hearths, into cloth, photographed
in thunderstorms, forest fires, waterfalls, and found
gentle in walls, the torn asbestos of a henhouse,
lichen of cathedrals.
                        But this is not enough.
There's the taste of dust churned up from a dirt road
a wrecked pickup has rattled down, late summer,
the dusk like cooling iced tea, almost too sweet,
and the truck's wake coaxing a crushed wing upward.
There is rippling lake light slowing, how blackbirds
coil far off like smoke, shadows of small clouds
sailing in the fields. Always, there is rain,
its slow coming on in a heavy, ticking stillness,
how it sounds on the old barn's dark tin roof
or dripping from trees afterwards, when steam
curves ghostly along the blacktop, and new skies

gather in puddles. There are paths followed
at dawn through grazed fields flaming with dew,
the paths worn smooth as the handles of old tools.
And fireflies floating through the night, brief smells
of plowed earth caught through diesel, or colors
of sundown fallen in the hills, the cool air
sharpened with coal smoke, dark coming early,
when something is found.

Marion Montgomery

The Second Year

He went down to the field of a morning
At the time when corn is a rabbit's-ear high,
But his heart flew on through the dawn-clear sky
With the crows he startled with his stoning.
And that was the first and the clearest warning.

She at the window could not know,
She turned to her work and sang as she did.

And he went down to the field of a morning
At the time when the corn was high as his belt.
The anxious cry of the crows, he felt,
Was somehow a laugh at his daylong burning,
Such was the canker. And such was the warning.

And she, with her mind on the life she warmed,
Hummed low songs toward a ripe full fall.

He went down to the field of a morning
When the heat-struck stalks rattled dry as brown bones
And the burnt field shimmered. The grasshopper drones
Fried in the air, and the crows, all disowning
The powder-dry field, had flown with the morning.

Alone she trimmed and stitched at a gown
In a house as quiet as a Monday church.

He went down through the field of a morning
When the leaves of the poplar flashed on the hill.
He turned at the edge and looked his fill
At the wind-blown stalks and the low house sunning,
And then he leaped the dry brook running,
On through the poplars into the morning.

She watched from the window, her fall at hand.

[129]

When night came down she set him a light.

But there was that within her eyes
One sees when the wild doe's stung to the heart
By the broad coarse head of a hunter's dart
And stands stock still before she dies
And dies with a wild hurt look in her eyes.

The wind blows soft through the bright dead leaves,
But winter's a word that still wants telling.

W. R. Moses

Old Theme

It seems disrespectful to Villon to put it so, but
Where are the cells of yesteryear?
Where are the teeth the bones the blood the gullet
Comfortably yours just seven years ago?
It isn't a light inquiry. One does not care
Into what sewer the snow ran, or into what bog;
But it isn't that way about the firmer flesh
And the twenty-twenty vision of twenty-two.

I remember, as a boy, by the water,
How the fish in the evening flashed silver
As they sloshed on the surface, playing or eating flies.
I do not think now of the gray-blue grace of the water,
Admire the aesthetic in fish, or else the athletic.
I recall instead that the scaly flashing resembled
Silver, durable metal.

It had not tarnished when, a long time later,
Evening dimmed over me and the same water.
I reflected that fish have even more tragedies
Than the nightingale Keats told lies about; each
Generation has always its sons spiked in its jaws.
But my teeth my bones my blood my gullet
Cried out that the rising, flashing fish resembled
Silver, durable metal.

Michael Mott

Don Juan in Winter

Women like mirrors yet who plot with Fate,
catch my grimace, return it still a smile,
darken your luster! I have learned to hate
what no return through you can reconcile.

My snares, my plots, take ribbons from your hair;
disguised as doves my crows are powdered things;
my flattering words have all their hindparts bare;
when I croak "Morning" all the orchard sings.

You enemy to sleep, dear What's-your-name?,
summon more play and have the loser's right.
Call off the pack! You have confused the game;
though I cheat still I fumble in plain sight.

My Hearts changed Spades chime on the frozen turf;
my Diamonds clump like coal the forest floor;
red spots lead huntsmen to some reeking earth;
black suits nailed grinning on a barnyard door.

Dear, clocks cluck time, cards fall like giant flakes.
Through that cloth arch, beyond the windows, lie
the parklands gray with dawn, the winter lakes
stacked with black antlers where beasts lock and die.

Lisel Mueller

Milkweed Pods in Winter

Months in the house have steamed them open:
wide, curved mouths
brimful of feathers,
as if speech had been held back
and wanted out, to fly
like those white surprises
when we speak in the frozen air
and our words appear
as weightless figures.

If this is speech, it is
the speech of silence: winter speech.
It is what we would say to each other
if we could find the heart,
if there were no music
to say it for us
and the appetite of our bodies
did not swallow language clean:
we would be like these milkweed pods,
overflowing.

Southpaw

Were you an only child? she asks.
No, but you've always favored the dreamer,
the star pitcher who writes novels,
the prophet with the red armband,
the low notes of the piano,
the swimmer against the stream.

You learned the truth early, that handles
are on the other side,
that doors are hinged to slow your entrance
and gloves and gadgets are made for others,
but you know that the ancient tools—
jugs, spoons, hammers, rakes—
care only about your opposable thumb.

It's your birthright, the extra effort
you've secretly come to love.
Left, left, the drill sergeant stutters
and you smile like one of the chosen.
You push the reluctant ballpoint
forward, while the letters wave back
and taste the word *sinister* on your tongue:
how enchanting it is, so sensuous,
the song of a sea-nymph with two left arms.

Howard Nemerov

A Cabinet of Seeds Displayed

These are the original monies of the earth,
In which invested, as the spark in fire,
They will produce a green wealth toppling tall,
A trick they do by dying, by decay,
In burial becoming each his kind
To rise in glory and be magnified
A million times above the obscure grave.

Reader, these samples are exhibited
For contemplation, locked in potency
And kept from act for reverence's sake.
May they remind us while we live on earth
That all economies are primitive;
And by their reservations may they teach
Our governors, who speak of husbandry
And think the hurricane, where power lies.

The Three Towns

The road from Adonoi to I Don't Know
Runs on, our elders say, to I Deny.
Whatever won't let us stop won't let us go.

The erected spirit, with its will to know,
Leaves the home town in its own good time to try
The slope from Adonoi to I Don't Know.

The slope so steep, it takes us who knows how
Further from God and closer to the sky;
Whatever won't let us stop won't let us go.

The elders warn, but it is always so:
The beautiful and brash are they that try
The road from Adonoi to I Don't Know

And sometimes in their brilliance mount up so
They wind up further on in I Deny;
Whatever won't let us stop won't let us go.

The clear Satanic eminence of How
Runs further to the hermitage of Why.
Whatever won't let us stop won't let us go;
The road from Adonoi? I just don't know.

John Frederick Nims

Finisterre

And yet a kiss, like blubber, 'd blur and slip,
Without the assuring skull beneath the lip.

So the scrivener quilled. In blurry *bluh*'s, such stuff
As charading the flab of flesh, with play enough
On that *kiss* and *skull* for a high sign: love and death
—Two which, the whole world over, catch our breath.
Perpending the two, he sorts their *is*, and *has*,
With many a resonant sequitur, such as:

No way to enfold the flesh and not feel bone.
No way: kiss flesh (poor thing) and you kiss alone.
There's no one home—not a soul. Tang, gusto, glow
Carouse in the skull: heaven's carousel of snow,
Good sleighing one Christmas Eve, Ghost Lake in Maine,
And what you did, age seven, in the rain
Under the maple's tent—no sensual hour
But had its glory in the bone-built tower.

"Tower! There's your old high-horse way! Folks below
Tell: it's a tackier shanty."

                    Even so,
Celebrate—sleek or tousled, in bow, béret,
Goldenhead, towhead, chestnut, raven, gray—
All the world's flurry in your thatchy hut
(There's nothing but old foodstuff in the gut).

Lay your head closer, love. It's world on world
When lips on, up, in, under lips are curled.
Like riding the primal lava!

                Some such flare

Rolling us, molten, to far Finisterre.
Before us, zodiacal sagas. On we grope,
To be spun in a spangling Nova—there's our hope!

To be spun, like the North's wild lovelocks, round the pole—
Space and time
              twirl immersing
                          soul in soul.

Joyce Carol Oates

Luxury of Sin

A white January sun on fire through the blinds,
giving a tropical heat.
Solitude. Silence. Infinite white walls.
Come here, the mirror whispers,
O come here: I promise you the world.

I am alone, I am a miracle, alone,
even the sun cannot touch me,
the maps are all blank, the white has spread,
Come here, the mirror whispers.

Gloating voluptuous in secret, the sin
of the empty mirror: the glass reflecting nothing:
only the vacant room, splendid
in vacancy.

I am alone, I am a miracle, unspeakable in luxury,
believe nothing else I have said,
the white winter sun is ablaze.

The miraculous, wrote Coleridge: I stretch out my arm!

The miraculous, claims the mirror: No one is here!

Mary Oliver

Skunk Cabbage

And now as the iron rinds over
the ponds start dissolving,
you come, dreaming of ferns and flowers
and new leaves unfolding,
upon the brash
turnip-hearted skunk cabbage
slinging its bunched leaves up
through the chilly mud.
You kneel beside it. The smell
is lurid and flows out in the most
unabashed way, attracting
into itself a continual spattering
of protein. Appalling its rough
green caves, and the thought
of the thick root nested below, stubborn
and powerful as instinct!
But these are the woods you love,
where the secret name
of every death is life again—a miracle
wrought surely not of mere turning
but of dense and scalding reenactment. Not
tenderness, not longing, but daring and brawn
pull down the frozen waterfall, the past.
Ferns, leaves, flowers, the last subtle
refinements, elegant and easeful, wait
to rise and flourish.
What blazes the trail is not necessarily pretty.

At Loxahatchie

All day
the alligators
lumbered into and out of
the water, herons

stood in the trees
combing their white shoulders,
vultures
floating just under the clouds

were in no hurry—
sooner or later
the mysterious circles
always closed.

I had dreamed of such a place,
but this was my first visit
to the thick parks and the state of mind
called Florida. Streams

wandered everywhere
among the shining mangroves.
At one I paused
to drink and inside me

the water whispered: *And now, like us,*
you are a million years old.
But at the same time
the enormous and waxy flowers

of the shrubs around me, whose names
I did not know,
were nodding in the wind and sighing:
Be born! And I knew

whatever my place in this garden
it was not to be what I had always been—
the gardener.
Everywhere the reptiles thrashed

while birds exploded into heavenly
hymns of dark song and the vultures
drifted like black angels and clearly nothing
needed to be saved.

Robert Pack

Trying to Separate

Please give me room, Howard! I've tried before
to tell you this—I have to leave you, oh
that came out wrong, there's no way I can find
the words that sound as if I'm making sense.
Not *you*, Howard, it isn't *you* I'm leaving,
it's Vermont, the starving deer, the spring
that never comes, the gloomy ice and clay.
Even when late sun lingers in the birches,
darkness fills my mind. I need more light,
more red—not just a pair of cardinals,
but flocks of them. There's no red in the earth;
purple spreads in the mountains when the sun
descends behind the hemlock trees as if
the animals were grieving there. And fall
comes much too soon, the yellows are too brief;
I don't have time here to forget myself.
I want to go to Tucson where I lived
before my mother died, where stones are red,
the desert light *feels* red—a gradual
slow, steady red. I need more time to dwell
on images I want to paint. Don't joke
again about my always *seeing red*!
You once said that my painting is the cause,
but that's not first; I need a different light
than you to *see*, and then the paintings come.
You need Vermont, you need an inward light;
you need the feeling that each day is hard.
Love cannot feed itself with love. We've tried.
Love needs something outside itself—children—
and we've delayed deciding that too long.
You said one only chooses children after
one has had them; then they become like *place*,
then they're the *given* like the landscape is.
You think there's got to be some deeper cause

[143]

for breaking up. I fear you may be right,
but I can't find that cause; Howard, believe me,
I've really looked. All that I know is red,
and you desire gray—punishing winter
is your season, white birches are your light.
You need Vermont to be yourself. You do!
Don't try to comfort me; don't touch me now—
that makes me angry when I want to talk—
for then you'll have a reason I should stay.
You'll say: admit it's *me* you want to leave,
admit you're angry, that it's not because
you love the goddamn red; you'll say we have our sunsets
blazing on the snow, we have our fire at night,
as if I'll give in like I always do.

Linda Pastan

The Printer

for Roland Hoover

Baskerville, Perpetua, Garamond:
I thought you were naming a dance,
but the only minuet is typeface moving
across the page, and you in your apron, bowing—
journeyman to the letter, apprentice to the word.
The smell of ink, like the smell of bread
signifies morning, a bleeding of color
at the horizon, the horizon itself
a line of boldface too distant to read.

In this world there are as many letters
as leaves, as birds, as flecks of ash;
whole armies of alphabets march across
margins of pavement, margins of snow.
Now there's a smudge on your forehead
where your hand strayed
making those architectural gestures,
the Pleasure of our Company is requested,
the ceremonial announcement of birth or death.

Your press is as fruitful as a wine press,
the sound of its motion like surf, hour after hour
reams of paper spreading their deckle-edged foam.
At night you distribute the type as carefully
as if you were placing your daughters in their beds.
Dark enters, a time before language,
but the sky is printed in white indelible stars,
with God's own signature—that thumbprint of moon,
like the printer's colophon
on heaviest Mohawk Superfine.

Epilogue

for J. I.

Years later the girl died
no longer a girl,
and the old man fishing
in sullied waters
saw his one mistake
flash by—
but only for a moment.
The moon continued
its periodic rise and fall,
sometimes the shape
of a snow elk's horn,
sometimes a vague
repository of light.
Katerina married
someone else.
Robert though only a minor character
grew into the hero
of another story.
And the house was rebuilt
by strangers.
Only the lake stayed the same,
its surface equivocal
as the pages of a book
on which everything remains
to be written.

Prologue

Nothing has happened yet.
The house settles
into its stones,
unoccupied;
the road curves
towards something—
away from something else.
A single elk bends
to the lake to drink,
or in the confusion of dusk
perhaps it is simply
an old tree
leaning over the water.
If there were voices
their language would be
expectancy; but the silence
is nearly perfect.
Even the sun is motionless
before it takes that definite plunge
into the darkness
of the first chapter.

Alice Golembiewski Phillips

The Rapture Is Coming

The frame church waits
By the tracks. I lean my shadow across the window,
Listen. My sister
The believer had told me, *the rapture
Is coming*. Voices swell out of air
Like a thin whistle rushing
To meet you and *light breaks*, she said,
Into a million pieces like stained glass.

She sits upright in the meeting room
And hears voices. She allows herself
No instruments, only the beating
Of hand against breast, hearts pounding
In the semidarkness around her.

Over the unforgiving country
A train rumbles, sounds
A long, low blast in warning.
It grows, looms
Like a man over a bed.
The worshipers lift their heads.
I straighten up.
The storm has passed and the rails die down.

Sister, I have sinned again and again
And found it good. Only lately
Has disappointment come to visit.
Forgive me. We travel
Our different roads into eternity,
The fanned-out smoke against the sky.

Stanley Plumly

Blossom

And after a while he'd say his head was a rose,
a big beautiful rose, and he was going to blow it
all over the room, he was going to blast blood.

And after a while he'd just put his head in his one good
hand the way children do who want to go into hiding.

I still can't get the smell of smoke from a woodstove out of my head.
A woman is frying bacon and the odor is char and sour and somebody
running a finger over your tongue. All those dead years and the grease

still glue on the wall. In Winchester, Virginia, the year the war
ended, the blacks were still dark clouds. My uncle had a knife
pulled on him holding his nose.

                      When the Guard marched eleven
German prisoners of war down from Washington they marched them
right through town, and it was spring and a parade like apple blossom.
Black and white, we lined up just to watch.

I still can't get the smell of apples out of my head—
trees in orchards all over the county, like flowers in a garden.
The trees the Germans planted that spring looked like flowers,

thin as whips. Even so the branch of a full-grown apple tree
is tested every summer: when I didn't watch I picked along with
every black boy big enough to lift a bushel. Frederick County.

The National Guard in nineteen forty-five was my father and any
other son who stayed home. Next door the father of my friend
had been home two long years, one arm, one leg gone. He was

honorary. He was white sometimes, and black, depending.
He was leaf and woodsmoke and leaning always into the wind.

And everybody called him Blossom because of the piece of apple
he kept tucked at one side of his mouth. When he was drinking
he'd bring his bottle over and talk to my father about Germans.

They go down, he'd say, they all go down on their guns.

Each five-petaled flower on the tree means an apple come summer.
I still can't get the bourbon smell of Blossom out of my head.
He spits his apple out and shoots himself in the mouth with his finger.

Bin Ramke

Martyrdom: A Love Poem

Each of the dozen saints is bound
to his own stake, like a prize
tomato. We know each death
will bear a flame-red fruit.

When necessity lugs us into another year
do not be misled by calendars: a new year
begins with each tick, each time you
remember time is passing. And what a pet
you've made with a numbered dial
around time's neck, a leash
of pendulum to walk it
once around the block before you sleep.
At night time gathers itself,
a pack of neighborhood dogs
to knock over your garbage cans
to gnaw your discarded secrets
scattered for the neighbors to see if they,
bothered by the noise, will look
at your small life withering
in the dew of the backyard grass.

You and I owe nothing to sanctity,
find there no help at all, nothing
so dangerous makes us what martyrs are—
we have visions of each other
in our sleep, we know the secrets,
we have touched each other's
intimate places. We love because
it grows late and the tomatoes
are ripening. A morning glory
climbs one stake, mingles with the crude

green-and-pink-striped fruit: tomorrow
we will look at what we've done.

Certainly I would die for you:
that is the easy part, like falling
from grace or off a log.

Syllogism

If every good boy deserves favor, and all cows eat grass,
then music, like milk, is made of sly croppings
of green blades glistening some mornings in dew
and desire, of the wish to be better and do more.

Nothing returns whole unless transformed.
The insinuant twitter of birds in the barn when the boy
does chores before school—these sounds will return
when his drink is stronger, his love of life weaker
perhaps, but better for being not duty but desire.

Sing something, solemn boy, and press your head deeply
into the flank of the cow while the music of milk
deepens in the bucket. All flesh is grass.

Byron Herbert Reece

Such Instance

A young girl took a walk
In the cool last hour of day
Among the stones of the graveyard.
A feathery spray
Of the sedge began to talk
And she cocked her head
And stood still, listening hard.
The low sedge said:

Being not beautiful
Nor here of any use
I am all ways condemned
And fire is set to my root
When frosts have nipped me dry.
Yet by dead flesh I am stemmed
And the gray stuff of a skull
When the flames begin to shoot
Flames, flames high
And bends to the wind's stroke
And passes in smoke.

The young girl trembling stood
With one foot lifted up,
Poised there about to flee
When out of the tulip's cup
Nearly the color of blood
The words came free:

With what cold constancy
Stare upon the sky
The dead who lack all sight!
From one of twin sockets I
Have sprung, the instrument
That once marked which way went

The sun, and which came night
Feeds me. And by its side
The other, gaping wide,
Forsaking its bony frame,
Sees nothing the same.

The young girl turned to flee
But her foot caught in the root
Of a stout, wide-branching tree;
The headstone at its foot
In syllables of stone
Spoke a name, her own.
There leaned, as if to read
The name, a tulip there;
Around its crimson cup,
Till faggot should confirm
The limit of its term,
The wavering sedge thrust up
Fine feathery tufts in air.

David Rigsbee

Crickets

They are without memory, making
up the night's story continually,
like Scheherazade. They are the old men
who pull the wool caps down
over their brows after the fashion
of railway baggage clerks.
They limp, paying no mind
to a missing leg. They crawl
in the bottom of bait buckets
knowing there is no exit.
When the grass grows thick
as the pile of a Persian rug,
and intoxicated with rain,
bully with heat, they are there
picking their way through tropical
forests. Then when night comes
and with it desire, and with it
love, and with it love's decline,
and with it death and the second death,
they take their place in the orchestra.

Pattiann Rogers

The Creation of the Inaudible

Maybe no one can distinguish which voice
Is god's voice sounding in a summer dusk
Because he calls with the same rising frequency,
The same rasp and rattling rustle the cicadas use
As they cling to the high leaves in the glowing
Dust of the oaks.

His exclamations might blend so precisely with the final
Crises of the swallows settling before dark
That no one will ever be able to say with certainty,
"That last long cry winging over the rooftop
Came from god."

Breathy and low, the vibrations of his nightly
Incantations could easily be masked by the scarcely
Audible hush of the lakeline dealing with the rocky shore,
And when a thousand dry sheaths of rushes and thistles
Stiffen and shiver in an autumn wind, anyone can imagine
How quickly and irretrievably his whisper might be lost.

Someone faraway must be saying right now:
The only unique sound of his being
Is the spoken postulation of his unheard presence.

For even if he found the perfect chant this morning
And even if he played the perfect strings to accompany it,
Still, no one could be expected to know
Because the blind click beetle flipping in mid-air,
And the slider turtle easing through the black iris bog,
And two savannah pines shedding dawn in staccato pieces
Of falling sun are already engaged in performing
The very same arrangement themselves.

Jay Rogoff

Teaching My Students Prosody

My mistress, when she walks, treads on the ground.

My hands have tried
conducting your eyes to follow feet, tried to lead
you fox-trotting through mysteries of scansion.
I've stooped: "Listen: it's got a good beat."

How can I skate you on this ice
shinier than the glaze upon your eyes,
and get your limbs to pump to organ music
until they can waltz to the pure swing of melody
and sing, sure of it?

Remember
the slowing pulse—
75—72—68—
numbering you to sleep
cradled in arms, a wrist beside your ear;

or the tapping in your chest
when you first knew a lie—
the smashed window or someone's "lost"
watch you stole—was contraband with which you could get away.

And getting away: feeling one heart race
in its bare chest on your bare chest
that holds the heart that syncopates upon that other,
both fluttering in a timeless quickstep
while, pounding, out in the parlor, the pendulum
tells your nerves each step your mother steps
as she trots home, springing, with some new shirts
she's picked out just for you, and the big clock
counts Stop Stop Stop Stop.

And suddenly it's you quickening the click of your
steps to the beat of your

[157]

blood, and clutching the shirts you bought for your
child, and—
today school gets out early.
(Remember counting, pushing
the tiny body bloodily out
and feeling, at last, relief.)

Stately dance
your daughter up the aisle, abandon her,
then glide
her in the final waltz that will elide
her from your arms forever.

Pace
the long steps following your father. Approach
the space,
and count your pummeling pulse. Confront
the coffin
with spade after spade after spade of dirt
until it leaves your glassy sight, in the only place
counting stops.

Reg Saner

Orchestra

The conductor's cocked twig turns out
to be a mountain hike through the kettledrum's buttered thunder
and a flute birdwatching our daydreams. Then tremolo
slurs the violin section's left fingers in unison
like sand lilies curled against wind.

Lull of bassoons, solo trumpet. And back to the bones
of this music we came for; we came to hear structure
but find the female bassist pretty; or pretty, considering.
And a strain colonizing us earlier as oboes
claims us again as trombones
flowing underground, past ore lying in veins
of solar gold like smashed cars, delving geodes of mineral skies,
white tie and tails, durable evening gowns
giving lessons by day, not making much money.

But we've come to follow album notes. Except for this sadness
hearing dull uncles, aunts, neighbors, second-hand cousins
tell us all they had meant to say,
this sadness at finding we love them
in the faces of strangers, the fog wrists of cellos
turning us into little wells of deep space,
pouring us into and out of our lives
like all we had meant them to be
if only we had remembered.

Penelope Scambly Schott

The rock of this odd coincidence

How these old hills flow down
beneath houses and roads and supermarkets,
down into the pool of evening,

only a small chip of a moon rising.

It will not do to speak of cities
nor how the flat cement
is crowding my grandfather's bones
in a square of sour dirt.

He said he remembered the Indian wars
and the edges of Chicago all cornfields.

Not on the trolley or the El
shrieking sparks in the night,
not in my grandfather's Model T's
or even the Packard I almost remember,
nobody goes back.

In the thin moonlight
I know how the heat of our star
is all spinning away:
the tidy woodpile scalloped in snow,
the diamond-faceted coal,
my own breath steaming.

To ask for reasons
merely presupposes reasons
here on this rock of odd coincidence
where none of us, no not one,
asked for these lives.

Philip Schultz

My Guardian Angel Stein

In our house every floor was a wailing wall
& each sideward glance a history of insult.
Nightly Grandma bolted the doors believing God

had a personal grievance to settle on our heads.
Not Atreus exactly but we had furies (Uncle Jake
banged the tables demanding respect from fate) & enough

outrage to impress Aristotle with the prophetic unity
of our misfortune. No wonder I hid behind the sofa sketching
demons to identify the faces in my dreams & stayed under

bath water until my lungs split like pomegranate seeds.
Stein arrived one New Year's Eve fresh from a salvation in Budapest.
Nothing in his 6,000 years prepared him for our nightly bacchanal

of immigrant indignity except his stint in the Hundred Years' War
where he lost his eyesight & faith both. This myopic angel knew
everything about calamity (he swore he taught King David the art

of hubris & Moses the price of fame) & quoted Dante to prove others
had it even worse! On winter nights we memorized the Dead Sea scrolls
until I could sleep without a night light & Saturdays went to movies

where he explained the Big Mysteries such as women (he was married
300 times & still played around & drunk on Sabbath wine went on
about a Hindu princess who'd punctured his self-esteem) & why

the stars appear only at night ("Insomniacs, they study the Torah
all day!"). Once I asked him outright: "Stein, why is our house
so unhappy?" Adjusting his rimless glasses, he said: "Boychick,

all humans are disappointed. Life is a comedy salted with despair.
So laugh yourself to sleep each night & with luck, pluck & credit cards

you'll beat them at their own game. Catharsis is necessary in this place!"

Ah, Stein, bless your outsized wings & balding pate & while I'm at it
why not bless the imagination's lonely fray with time, which, yes,
like love & family romance, has neither beginning, middle nor end!

Bettie M. Sellers

If Justice Moved

Dante had the right idea,
consigning traitors
to the deepest pits of Hell—

you, traitor with beard scarcely
formed, belong in ice confined
or gnashed by Satan's bloody teeth.

The master poet limned no woman
more betrayed than Dido was—
no lines depict a bitter face like mine . . .

You mowed my grass, spread sandwiches
at my kitchen table. Nights,
you smudged tears with dirty knuckles.

I trusted you to tend my child
and you have left her bleeding,
limp as the stuffed tiger

empty-eyed in his jungle.
If I understood, I could forgive—
but, seeing her, I'd give my chance

at Heaven to take up Ugolino's place.
If Ruggiero's neck be yours—
I'd gnaw on it a thousand years.

Anne Sexton

The Witch's Life

When I was a child
there was an old woman in our neighborhood
whom we called The Witch.
All day she peered from her second-story window
from behind the wrinkled curtains
and sometimes she would open the window
and yell: Get out of my life!
She had hair like kelp
and a voice like a boulder.

I think of her sometimes now
and wonder if I am becoming her.
My shoes turn up like a jester's.
Clumps of my hair, as I write this,
curl up individually like toes.
I am shoveling the children out,
scoop after scoop.
Only my books anoint me,
and a few friends,
those who reach into my veins.
Maybe I am becoming a hermit,
opening the door for only
a few special animals?
Maybe my skull is too crowded
and it has no opening through which
to feed it soup?
Maybe I have plugged up my sockets
to keep the gods in?
Maybe, although my heart
is a kitten of butter,
I am blowing it up like a zeppelin.
Yes. It is the witch's life,
climbing the primordial climb,

a dream within a dream,
then sitting here
holding a basket of fire.

Locked Doors

For the angels who inhabit this town,
although their shape constantly changes,
each night we leave some cold potatoes
and a bowl of milk on the windowsill.
Usually they inhabit heaven where,
by the way, no tears are allowed.
They push the moon around like
a boiled yam.
The milky way is their hen
with her many children.
When it is night the cows lie down
but the moon, that big bull,
stands up.

However there is a locked room up there
with an iron door that can't be opened.
It has all your bad dreams in it.
It is hell.
Some say the devil locks the door
from the inside.
Some say the angels lock it from
the outside.
The people inside have no water
and are never allowed to touch.
They crack like macadam.
They are mute.
They do not cry help

except inside
where their hearts are covered with grubs.

I would like to unlock that door,
turn the rusty key
and hold each fallen one in my arms
but I cannot, I cannot.
I can only sit here on earth
at my place at the table.

Snow

Snow,
blessed snow,
comes out of the sky
like bleached flies.
The ground is no longer naked.
The ground has on its clothes.
The trees poke out of sheets
and each branch wears the sock of God.

There is hope.
There is hope everywhere.
I bite it.
Someone once said:
Don't bite till you know
if it's bread or stone.
What I bite is all bread,
rising, yeasty as a cloud.

There is hope.
There is hope everywhere.
Today God gives milk
and I have the pail.

Charles Simic

Severe Figures

If Death and Liberty
Can be personified,
Why not History?

It's got to be a fat old man
In faded overalls
Outside a house trailer
On a muddy road to some place called Pittsfield
    or Babylon.

He draws the magic circle
So the chickens can't get out,
Then he hobbles to the kitchen
For the knife and pail.

Today he's back carrying
A sack of yellow corn.
You can hear the hens cluck,
The young cocks strut their stuff.

Cathy Smith-Bowers

The Fat Lady Travels

On any train
she is the occupant
of either seat—
no hopes for a handsome stranger,
no petty arguments
as to who
will get the window
or the aisle.
She gets them both.

When she dreams,
she is never the goddess
turning men to pigs.
She is the pig.
She is the one gross eye
of the Cyclops
fending off the spears
of her disgrace.

She is all of Brobdingnag.

Her green dress blowzes
in the halcyon wind.
She is turgid water
flooding the station,
home for leviathans.

What she should lose
would be enough
to make the sister
she never had,

and how thin
the both of them would be
gliding on fine-point skates
across some fragile pond

and, oh, it holding!

Dave Smith

Caravati's Salvage: Richmond, Virginia

He's the reaper, the buyer, the keeper of grand houses
gone to pieces, and the choice parts are here.
You want big doors, brass knobs, stained glass?
A hand-carved knocker? Grandfather clock? Chandeliers?

Maybe those shutters that lined Monument Avenue,
heartwood, the paint age-blistered, kept closed
a decade, some of them, when Lee died? Or you
desire staircase, railing, marble mantels, bellows—

he's stacked it all in heaps high as a pile of guns.
Ask. Caravati keeps. Endless old names, how they lived.
Eighty-three now, hair white as nightgowns in the sun,
he'll guide you, touching each piece, a boy you'd give

a nickel to, in your foyer, stiffened by his bell,
trembling at his words. How still he stands like delight.
He offers water, a beaded jar, from his well.
The one his fathers dug. Way down, and still sweet.

Jordan Smith

For Dulcimer & Doubled Voice

Because the sadness of the mode rests
    in empty singing between the strings; because
        to have this body's close-knit grain, split heart
of cherry, chambered and echoing, is knowledge
    even the deepest songs barely graze our hands,
        whorls slipping away in quiet water
as the bass dive; because the reflections
    of trees lace gray shallows, the pitch and cry
        of marsh light as it quavers, fades, in birch
trunks, sycamore, wooded fretwork marking
    our channel's twisted course; the shores you trace
        beyond us in the haze keep their distance,
vanish, low drone of loss beneath our strokes.
    Silent chorus before the water breaks,
        the quill fallen on the burnished soundboard,
this is ground and air of the river's chant:
    wind turns in the reeds, you tune the dulcimer's
        one doubled chord, and what seemed rooted
in the pattern of vines along these banks
    is undercut by the current's mirrored
        division of each leaf: dissonance
of wake and passage. I watch my image sharpen,
    flare, drifting glaze of sun, a sorrow borne
        away like waves, encircling, spreading outward,
beyond what I have left, the body taken
    at last under the keeping of your song.
        If I trust these bearings, if I follow
the white runs as you play, where would we be
    but here, wound in tendrils of the willow,
        you leading my hands along lines of bark,
watersheds passing into watercourses,
    backwaters, as the tree lifts from the minor
        dark of roots, stream, and burdened sky

to a key where no element is natural
        that does not shift its nature. Curled refrain
            of fog, curved, polished resonance in old wood,
these gestures of grace carry us, and are gone,
        our movement so reflected in the eddying
            distances of the marsh, we seem always
to have just fallen still. As a melody
        repeated on itself becomes the ground
            of silences, as a chart read in scaled
floorboards, in soundings of air, maps a course
        already beneath the hull, we have startled
            a heron from her nest in the cattails,
and can only watch her pass, blue and dun pinions
        spread, until the scudding of dunes and river
            is netted in her flight, forgotten, her cry
driven past a line of sand at the harbor's mouth.
        As we glide through slow water toward the dock.
            Because this is what we're brought to in intervals
of waves: woods and landings; because the current
        flowing toward us and back is a promise
            that what we touch becomes us at last,
moments of song, these splinters swirling
        together in the dulcimer shape of two lovers
            and apart; because we know our lives in the fall
and swell of strings, a sad tuning, still and changed
        to this beauty that gives rise only to itself:
            rings of water, rings of bark, our faces
turning closer; because that is enough.

Elizabeth Spires

The Travellers

We have black teeth but we dream just the same
as the people who live in houses.
 (Quoted in *Irish Tinkers* by Janine Wiedel & Martina O'Fearadhaigh)

When the lake lies still as a mirror,
giving the sky back every star it has stolen,
when the moon bleaches our nightclothes
white as the shirts that flutter in store windows,
when fog erases the walls you have built,
stone by stone, to keep us out,
                                    then we will come,
driving our wagons through your painted dreams,
entering your houses on tiptoe.
We've brought the tin cup
you never bought from us, a penny
for your tongue since you like the taste
of money. We've brought our daughters and sons,
the dead ones, who whisper and sing
as they go through your children's playthings.
They beg us to stay awhile, saying
they are cold and want to drink all the milk
they can hold. But we are travellers.
We know it's bad luck taking the dead on the road.
We'll leave them here, stopping again
in a year or a week or tomorrow.

You wake up sweating, feverish.
Your blankets are gone, all the windows
in your house are open.
You will never catch us.
We have taken the crooked road
to the next county, the trees hurrying
us along, pointing *this way, this way*,
with their crooked arms.
But the little ghosteens stay on,

hiding in closets and cupboards, whispering:
We are the rag and bone.
We are the summer walkers of the long acre.
We've come to pick the potato eyes
out of the quality folk,
to comb the gristle out of the meat
of the country men.

Carl L. Stach

The Final Prospect

Who among us would accept
that first day our progenitors
pondered a star, fixed it
between two others,
made gods of all three
and thus set out to tame the wilderness
that wails inside. And who would have it,
could we choose, that we should feel the need
to sleep when November's winds bend the trees'
backs to breaking, and leaves become
small memories that rattle across certain roads
and rooftops. Even so, some close out the cold
unwittingly, drink too late
on dark afternoons, take solace
in the condemnation of gods and fortune,
while others instead choose the voices
of children, the steam of large meals
and breathing covering their house windows,
obscuring the winter's light; until
the least of these awakes to find, like
a basketful of birds, his house
full of treachery, his life
moving forth; for while no one
was watching, he inherited the earth.

William Stafford

Trusting Each Other

Right at the height of the storm we crawled
where a ditch was, and looked out. Pieces
of our schoolhouse roof peeled off and sailed
overhead. We had to be low; we needed
the earth: even to walk was too proud.
We never saw any heroes after that.

And all winter we knew we were being watched.
Not proud, when we followed a trail we carried
a little clod from its beginning, a piece
of dirt, to be placed at the end: our part,
we knew, was—Remember. Were we afraid?
Yes. We knew someday we would be noticed again.

Now each of us knows that the other will keep
certain ways, for the faith: there is part of the world
not ever given over. Over to what?—to just wind,
to just what comes at the time. Now, wherever
the other one is, a certain measure is.
Say we are climbing a dangerous mountain:
we may only find the exact place to turn back,
but that can be triumph—not just reaching the top.

Lost where space is, we wander now, looking
for time, but we know:—it is folded into everything past.

It is following us.

Tides

The first wave of a new tide hardly
announces itself; but brothers and sisters
confirm that a mighty wave is coming,
and far from shore, bulging in mountain
ranges of ponderous water, the full
universe of the tide leans toward land.

Or winter beginning to move comes
that way, the sun withholding its full
afternoon blessing, a night when frost
creeps out; bones of the glacier
shift and get ready for the powerful surge
when what waits in the sky or mountain descends.

Even inside a cliff, inside that blind
forehead that fronts the ocean, a tide,
or winter, pulses in the gray body
of an earth too slow to respond but thrilled
into being and held in its crystal self,
a jewel of dull intensity inside the stone.

Gerald Stern

My Swallows

For hours I sit here facing the white wall
and the dirty swallows. If I move too much
I will lose everything, if I even breathe
I'll lose the round chest and the forked tail
and the nest above the window, under the ceiling.

As far as shame, I think I have lived too long
with only the moonlight coming in to worry
too much about what it looks like. I have given
a part of my mind away, for what it's worth
I have traded half of what I have—

I'll call it half—so I can see these smudges
in the right light. I think I live in ruins
like no one else, I see myself as endlessly
staring at what I lost, I see me mourning
for hours, either worn away with grief

or touched with simple regret, but free this time
to give myself up to loss alone. I mourn
for the clumsy nest and I mourn for the two small birds
sitting up there above the curtains watching—
as long as I am there—and I mourn for the sky

that makes it clear and I mourn for my two eyes
that drag me over, that make me sit there singing—
or mumbling or murmuring—at the cost
of almost everything else, my two green eyes,
my brown—my hazel, flecked with green and brown—

and this is what I'll do for twenty more years,
if I am lucky—even if I'm not—I'll live
with the swallows and dip through the white shadows
and rest on the eaves and sail above the window.

This is the way I *have* lived, making a life

for more than twenty years—for more than forty—
out of this darkness; it was almost a joy,
almost a pleasure, not to be foolish or maudlin,
sitting against my wall, closing my eyes,
singing my dirges.

Hidden Justice

This is my forest now, this Christmas cactus,
stretching out leaf after leaf,
pink blossom after pink blossom.
This is where I'll go to breathe
and live in darkness
and sit like a frog, and sit like a salamander,
and this is where I'll find a tiny light
and have my vision
and start my school—
in this dry and airy place
beside these trunks
in this fragrant mixture.

I will put my small stage here
under a thick leaf
and I will eat and sleep and preach right here
and put my two dogs there
to keep my two guards busy
with prayer and feeding.
I will live completely for the flowering,
my neck like a swan's,
my fingers clawing the air
looking for justice;
year after year the same,
my fingers clawing the air for hidden justice.

Alex Stevens

In Scorching Time

Note how the desert takes form, easily as wax. It moves
with light, and also with whatever on or above the surface
has scale or wing or claw. There are shadows and impressions, then,
from vulture, lizard, and toad. And big cactuses that seem
firm as thoughts do in the head's acre (and just as thorny):
if you draw closer you will find that, far from solid,
this one is riddled with sockets, with eyes
of small birds that roost in a castle
defended by spikes, complete with turrets and spires.

And of the sand—let me tell you how it swings
in tides so slow they defeat the mind,
great hinges of gravity for a door you expect to be pulled open
to reveal within. And how one seed, hard and round,
caught in the undulations here, may wait
one hundred brown-edged years for rain.
                                        Yes, but
I wanted to say more about seeds, how the seeds of all things,
if they stay anywhere, rest here. For often when I slept
in the desert, I would dream of a sky like this,
but of a different substance, and of a sand whose image
always shimmered in the moon, beyond this sand,
and then, on waking, I still partly held
those other visions, like shadows of the day's true marrow,
before fire spread in the brass sky
and burned up the residue like cobwebs.
                                        Seeds,
that was what I wanted to tell you of, how
the one wet trigger during as many years
as would make three of my lives to date,
reduces that encapsuled patience
to nothing (which was nothing all along, anyway, lost
even to the hawk's superb eye), except, perhaps,

as an image of some past state which stubbornly clings
between the roots and branches of the growing network,
something that struggles to hold life in the spaces of ours,
and that someday, when the sands turn over, will resume sway.

Mark Strand

A Story You Know

You dreamed all night of waking, of turning
to the window, and now
it is morning and the moon
sinks into the sea
and stars in the first light fade.
At the water's edge you stare at your shadow,
the ash of yourself falling away
into the dark of something you've known
but cannot remember.
You feel your days are like a dream
in the cold element of sleep,
that you have come only as far as your waking.
Your arms at your sides, your palms
to the wind, you try to imagine
what pocket of air will take your breath
and hold it awhile. Friend,
it is a story you know
of the man who wakens too soon
and goes to the water,
who turns and sees the sun
but not how gold it shines upon his face.

Lucien Stryk

Savants

Their hour had come
and gone: notions
blueprinted, years

of infinite zeros,
halved, quartered,
atomed for this day—

test-tubes of dust
measured to shake the
world. Now it was

done. Reaming traces
from their nails,
scattering like rocks

they'd blasted from
the earth, they turned
to raking gardens,

lecturing on peace,
regrets black-signatured
across an ashen page.

Secret codes unlearnt,
they crawled back to the
past on hands and knees.

Dyan Sublett

Simple Rituals

Everywhere the habits of late afternoon are repeated: birds circle above the street, a woman cups her hands over tea. She glances at the paper. In someone else's country soldiers wander the back roads, blowing holes through the forest. Here is a picture of ordinary men, dark ties loosened. One pulls off his glasses, rubs his eyes with a slow, grave motion. Reasonable words are spoken, words that do not sound like a mother screaming the name of her son from the bushes. It is the end of the day. The man who pulled off his glasses turns to no one in particular. War has a curious affinity with the letter *h*, he says. Hiroshima, holocaust, hydrogen. Help.

Never is the scent of japonica mentioned, how the Japanese formally welcome each season with poetry, a change of color in the children's kimonos. The thoughts of the woman drift this way, listening to a man raking leaves under the open window. His rake, the movement of his arms, is a small, insistent weight upon the air.

Something about the movement of the man disturbs her. The woman reaches out to close the window. Her shawl drops away from the tender inside of her arm, where there are pinmarks left from the needles drawing blood. The doctor teased about her blood running slow in this vein—it took so long to draw maybe she was afraid maybe she was trying to hold some back! Nothing was wrong with her, he said. The needles left two blue bruises the color of morning glories.

The woman knows nothing about death except that it will be an absence, which is the same way she thinks of the future. In her bedroom pelicans are painted on a silk screen in silver and red to bring luck in life. It is fall in Japan precisely when the texture of the screen yields to her fingers.

She trusts what she can touch, remembering the man who astonished her with the simple idea that her breasts were beautiful. She believed touching could save her from the small deaths that go undetected and so enjoyed the search of his hands and laughed when he bit the diamond stud from her ear. It was the kind of moment that arrives just after a light has been switched off, after the paper is laid down. It has nothing to do with the future.

Mary Swander

Novena

Eye of potato, thin neck of cabbage
arching out of the ground, I kneel
here in late April

and sprinkle ash on roots and stems.

Ash of oak, ash of pine, ash of elm
sifting into the dirt, paper ash,

ash to keep moths from drilling through
    the leaves,
ash to keep stalks from curling up,
     slinking away.

Ash of ash
blown down in a storm, logs sawed and split,

logs I carry in my arms,
while the warm ash waits through the winter,
sinking to the bottom of the stove.

Ash like snow, like skin.

Cool ash loose in the house at night,
settling in my lungs
as I sleep,

as I walk out into the dark,
a bucket of ash in my hand.

And in the morning,
my face on the pillow in ash.

David Swanger

What the Wing Says

The wing says, "I am the space behind you,
a dent in the fender, hands you remember
for the way they touched you. You can look
back and song will still throb. I am air
moving ahead, the outermost edge of desire,
the ripple of departure and arrival. But

I will speak more plainly: you think you are
the middle of your life, your own fulcrum,
your years poised like reckonings in the balance.
This is not so: dismiss the grocer of your soul.
Nothing important can be weighed, which is why
I am the silver river of your mornings and
the silver lake curled around your dark dreams.
I am not wax nor tricks stolen from birds.

I know you despair at noon, when sky overflows
with the present tense, and at night as you lie
among those you have wronged; I know you have failed
in what matters most, and use your groin to forget.
Does the future move in only one direction?
Think how roots find their way, how hair spreads
on the pillow, how watercolors give birth to light.
Think how dangerous I am, because of what I offer you."

Dennis Trudell

Green Tomatoes

Our eye pupils are always honest.
Death is the eye pupils
widening until that's all there is. Even the future,
even that young girl with the purple jersey
and a psychiatrist worried about tomorrow, even the eel
my son thought he saw in our lake
will vanish like last week's
circumference of green tomatoes.
All this movement around me is a flow toward death.
Therefore many feel
they must regard time like a trough.
But if death is an explosion of all our cells,
eh?, if death is an explosion outward
to join the cosmos like an idea
tentacles outward in all directions from its source
in a human brain, and a mouth moves,
a hand reaches out, cautiously,
or sailing like a fat gull,
like a porpoise, toward a breast or holster . . .
Eh? If death is a shoehorn
and everything we don't know is the foot . . .
Or a fulcrum—death is where we
finally balance history and birth.
I'm sitting in a drugstore
trying to write a revolutionary poem.
But old people keep getting older, rolled-up sleeves
keep passing nearby, keep fading
whether I can see it or not, keep straining
to weave air between their threads, to become dust.
And now that old woman with hair like a dead shirt
has said my name, has asked me
between its letters
if she is still alive . . .

Watch Them Die

Our brothers and mothers and cousins with strangers between their
syllables,
with time leaking out of their genitals. Our neighbors
with trouble filling their plates, with our uncles
and our favorite bus drivers
calling to us in our dreams, bringing
their parents' malignant cysts to our Thursdays, to premenstrual
depressions.
And our birthdays passing too quickly, like shuffled cards;
our summers tilting the lakes inside us, emptying them
into the lovely arc
between the seas and the sky, the sky and seas
replenished and cleansed by the rivulets of dead kidneys and spleens,
of broken houses, colors of rugs, of picture puzzles, of wedding
dresses . . .
Our sisters and their fathers and their brothers and the strangers
in their sweat
in factories producing the gears for our comforts,
and the poor standing in lines for their names,
and the mother-in-law arriving, again without warning,
with her gift-wrapped box of loneliness—
joining the horizontal totem pole outside our walls,
the pole of faces we can't turn away from,
the faces that know they have the right
to ask us to watch them die.

Charles Vandersee

Spring at Arm's Length

Leaning out of my Boston window
hearing the winos arguing,
I realize this is spring.

Nothing convinces me like these voices,
not the trees in small green flames
nor the pink unretouched arms

of women who've grown younger
in long sleeves and vinyl boots
all winter, but now in spring

leap, leap toward age.
The winos stay sleeved and stained
and gray all seasons.

In winter they find furnace rooms,
spring-cleaning niches in buildings
held up by walls of other buildings,

and, like rivers under ice, do not exist.
But brushes prickle walks; it's spring.
It's spring when the winos

come flapping against the curbs
and take hold of benches,
and curse each other and inflation.

Curse is the life force;
so is the bagged bottle going around,
life by ritual, life. . . .

As for me, I'm through
with my discovery and coffee break,

through shortly with temptation.

This is a disease ceremony,
like factory labor, wrong to celebrate,
but a gift. A gift to look in the mouth.

Ellen Bryant Voigt

A Fugue

for Tom Moore

1.

The body, a resonant bowl:
the irreducible gist of wood,
that memorized the turns
of increase and relinquishing:
the held silence
where formal music will be quarried
by the cry of the strings,
the cry of the mind,
under the resined bow.

2.

The deaf listen
with compensatory hands,
touching the instrument.
Musicians also
listen, and speak, with their hands.

Such elemental implements.
The eye trains on a grid of ink,
and the fingers quicken,
habitual, learnéd,
to recover the arterial melody.

3.

The long habit of living
ill disposes us to dying.
In this measured space,
a drastic weeping.

*

Music depends
on its own diminishing.
Like the remembered dead,
roused from silence
and duplicated, the song heard
is sound leaving the ear.

*

Medicine too is a temporal art.
Each day, children
are rendered into your keeping.
And so you take up your instruments
to make whole, to make live,
what others made.

4.

Pure science:
the cello in your lap;
the firm misleading bodies
of your own children
in your brother's room.
His illness is adult, and lethal.
You place the bow
and Beethoven turns again
from the stern physician
to annotate the page:
cantabile—
          meaning
not birdsong, windsong,
wind in the flue, bell, branch,
but the human voice,
distinct and perishable.

And you play for him.

David Wagoner

The Art of Surrender

To be wiped out to the last man would mean missing
All the advantages of giving up.
If you're outmaneuvered and wounded,
Deserted and surrounded,
Act out the painless protocol of surrender:
Your weapons handed over (apparently)
To the apparent victor.
Dignity. Your signature. Heads up, not off.

The winner is also giving up, remember:
No longer struggling with you, no longer winning
But, having prevailed,
Responsible now for all your worldly goods
And (he won't know it yet) your worldly evils.
The full-scale miseries of conquerors
Are yours to deliver
Discreetly with a vengeance from then on.

You must pay the strictest attention, but not attract it,
Must always be one of those far back in the chorus
Droning his praise off-key,
Replastering walls with long-in-the-sweet-tooth slogans
To his greater and grosser glory,
Shaking, not spears, but those more deadly banners
That will spur him onward
And downward through his hope to outdo the dead.

Then, gentle assassins, help him play the god
And gather near for his command performance.
He will search for love
In your deplorable eyes, but he won't find it
Where he thought it was: at his mercy. Your judgment then
May be more speechless, courtly, and merciless
Than his in a courtyard.
So much for any enemy. He's all yours.

[194]

Marilyn Nelson Waniek

It's All in Your Head

for Deborah M.

How easily my heart falls back into habits:
a little stress, and I'm checking my pulse again
for irregular beats.
Just last year I went once a week
to the emergency room,
afraid my breath would expand
the radiant pain in my chest.
I lay among the hurt, the dying,
checking my symptoms off on a mental list.

I didn't die; I napped
on the spotless stainless-steel beds.
I went home chastened, humble,
to the steeplechase of my life.
Now, like a bass drum dropped down the stairs,
my heart wakes me up again at night.
I pretend I'm not afraid
of the funeral procession
coming to order under my ribs.

I wanted to twirl a baton
in the 2082 parade.
The day Mrs. Gray predicted fame for me
the sixth-grade class dissolved
to an image of high-stepping white boots.
But I stumble after, out of step,
as the band strikes up with a hymn
and the colored congregation
slowly begins to move.

The trombone fades into the distance
with the flattened-out trumpets and drums;
the women carry black parasols:

Diverne, Annie, Ray, Mary, Charlie,
Geneva, Oneida, Zilphia, Blanche,
in shabby shoes and black straw hats
rescued from the backs of their closets.
Dark dresses reserved for such occasions
flicker around their calves.

Their felt fedoras in their hands,
their collars too white,
their heads small
with new haircuts, my grandfathers
and uncles walk in the bright morning.
Pete has taken off his white apron,
John, his overalls. Melvin, Rufus, Pomp,
in shiny shoes and suits, march
with Mister Tyler and the women.

I limp behind in my black hole shoes,
my hair crocheted with tangles
as it was when I was ten.
But my old heart groans
when the brass light from the tuba
takes the road that winds up the hill.
I hear the sisters ahead of me
join in a church-house moan
as the band ascends into the blues.

The moan changes
to a full-throated song,
a melody vaguely familiar,
though they're too far away now
for me to hear more than snatches.
I hum along with them,
halting, out of sync,
like a jay
in a tree full of finches.

It's jazz I hear now from the heights,
hands clap a rhythm like approaching rain.

I want so much to be a part of that music,
but I fall back again and again,
damned impossible stone.
By the time I pant up the narrow ridge
they took to the summit,
only the thin voice of a clarinet
rises from small blacks and lights.

It's not time yet to follow them over
from the top of my birthdate
to the other side of the dash,
where I'll be welcomed with fanfare.
This syncopation's only a habit
my heart has picked up
so I march back home
to the business of putting on clothes
and taking them off.

Robert Penn Warren

Seasons

1. *Downwardness*

Under ledges of snow outthrust from ledges
Of stone, once ledges of ice, water swells black
With white whirlpools of sputum at edges.
At the edge of the forest I have seen the year's first bear track.

Downstream, a high outthrust of snow groans, loses structure,
Falls in a smother and splash of white water boiling—
But not from heat. Boulders go grudging and grinding in rupture,
And one, heaved in air, chimes like a bell in that moiling.

After that tumult your ears with silence are tingling.
But no, not silence. Your ears deceive.
Yes, listen! What seemed such silence is only the singing
Of a thousand driblets and streamlets that receive

Stored snow-waters, ice-waters, earth-waters, freed now in season
On the vast mountain, where they even explore
The most secret channel a root drills in its deep personal reason.
Here gravity is the only god, and water knows no more

Than the lust for downwardness, and the deepest coil.
But time will change, clouds again draw up buckets, day-
light glitter in the highest leaf like green foil,
And in earth-darkness moisture will climb the lattices of clay.

All night we now hear the desperate downwardness.
All day we have watched the last icicle
Drip, drop by drop, as though from a wound—grow less and less.
Dark comes again. Shut eyes, and think of a sacred cycle.

II. *Interlude of Summer*

Even in the spruce-dark gorge the last
Fringe of ice is in fatal deliquescence,
And rising waters rise to shoulder a boulder past.
Green will soon creep back in white's absence.

Each day, at mathematically accelerated pace,
The yet-unseen sun will flood the eastern notch
With crimson, and you pick up a shoe, and yawn, and face
The morning news-screen of the world's hotch-potch or bloody botch.

Evening by evening, the climactic melodrama of
Day flares up from beyond the blackening silhouette
Of the mountain for the majestic pyre of
What of the day you can remember, or forget.

Later and later, each day, the eastern notch is now flooded
By dawn, and eyes gaze vacantly at the world's disaster
With customary indifference, for you know fate is hooded.
The woodland violet that was your love is replaced by the roadside aster.

The faces of the children are now hardening toward definition.
Your own life seems to lose definition, as it did last year.
But garden and grape arbor have fulfilled your ambition,
And gullet has sucked juice from the golden and tooth-gored pear.

An old friend dies this summer, and now whose carefully
Composed letters will challenge you? Your health is good. Conversation
Turns to New England foliage, which has begun beautifully.
We might come back for a weekend of delightful observation.

After all, aesthetics is a branch of philosophy.

[199]

Muted Music

As sultry as the cruising hum
Of a single fly lost in the barn's huge, black
Interior, on a Sunday afternoon, with all the sky
Ablaze outside—so sultry and humming
Is memory when in barn-depth, eyes shut,
You lie in hay, and wonder if that empty, lonely,
Muted music is all the past was, after all.
Does the past now cruise your empty skull like
That blundering buzz at barn-height, a region dim
Except for the window at one gable, where
Daylight is netted gray with cobwebs, and the web
Dotted and sagged with blunderers that once could cruise and hum?

What do you really know
Of that world of decision and
Action you once strove in? What
Of that world where now
Light roars, while you, here, lulled, lie
In a cunningly wrought and mathematical

Box of shade, and try, of all the past, to remember
Which was *what, what which.* Perhaps
That sultry hum from the lone bumbler cruising high,
In shadow, is the only sound truth makes,
And into that muted music you soon sink
To hear at last, at last, what you have strained for
All the years, and sometimes at dream-verge thought

You heard—the song the moth sings, the babble
Of falling snowflakes (in a language
No school could teach you), the scream
Of the reddening bud of the oak tree

As the bud bursts into the world's brightness.

[200]

Rosanna Warren

Painting a Madonna

If he has been so careful
in drawing the jointure of wrist and still childlike hand
    it is because
he himself does not quite believe

    in the spirit.
And yet, what else could account
    for the pale
dome of her brow, for flesh so fragile that

    it yearns toward
translucence like the veil which floats
    over her
calligraphic curls? He could almost see

    the Incarnation
as a trick of light. And maybe
    it was, radiance
so preoccupying her body she gave birth to

    its source. Still,
pigment is mineral, canvas is woven
    thread, the painter's
hand, as it moves, a machine of muscles and bone.

    Our daughter finds
she, too, has fingers, fingers! and grasps
    at grass, closing,
unclosing her tiny, definite fists, stained green.

    Around us, the garden
labors: the vine surges into the grapes, the tree
    bows over as if
worshiping its own pears, a column of ants

      minutely dismembers
the fledgling fallen among weeds. Our air
      drowses in scents
of linden, lavender, decay. Like Thomas,

      we have
to touch to believe. So the madonna, bent
      over her sleeping
child, strokes with one finger the insect bite marring

      His brow. She is watching
Him die. And now, for the first time, feels
      her own death stir
like a second child within her, and love, which we call the soul.

Michael Waters

The Faithful

Sometimes, when the world
no longer seems capable of surprise,
when your wife rehearses
the usual gestures of affection

and birches offer their annual
assortment of autumn leaves,
you forget how small the heart
might be, how fragile.

One morning, rushing to work,
you brush past a stranger
more beautiful than the dark
bruise of adolescence—

your fingers tracing a breast
at fourteen, your tongue
blooming with the moisture
on your sweetheart's throat—

and the world fashions a frail
shell, a pale rind,
the air within billowing
with the scent of buds unfolding,

so that in the story
you'll tell tonight to your children,
the cobbler in a barren country
lets fall his apron

to find, not nails, but
breathing, miraculous roses.

David Weiss

On the Marshes at Dawn

This is a prayer
unspoken as the sowing of seeds,

crossing great emptiness
like a wedge of geese splitting the dark air

under storm clouds, high above,
offered to a memory of trouble, to no one, to one other.

I am praying only for what's imaginable,
for an intimate, unreachable thing

that each day seems a footstep
further away, harder to get to.

But I say *wheat*
and a breeze bends it over or soon will.

I say *geese*
and already some are nesting in the cattails.

I say these words
and, like that, you are among them,

emerging as if from shadows
of laurel and stout cedars

as the world, drawing new breath
in the blueness of dawn,

holds it, briefly,
before the day-long sigh.

Norman Williams

The Tremors at Balvano

6 December 1980

The animals, that day, behaved with odd foreboding;
The hens refused their coops, and disgruntled swine
Upset their trays and rooted up their pens—
Toward evening, as the cobbled streets grew thick
With Romeos decked out in their *abitos de sera*,
The lightbulb strings began to tilt, and rumblings
Filled the stairwells, the galleries and porticos,
Like muttered news of scandal. The earth then shook
As sharply as a horse's flank nagged by summer flies,
And stone stacked centuries ago, the church and hillside huts,
Came down. Throughout that long and grieving night,
The villagers, the wise-ass boys and drunkard men,
The sturdy wives whose furrowed faces seemed to map
The yellow land, pulled out barely breathing bodies
By the arms, and as they worked the word went out
Of various astonishments, of a skimming village clerk
Thrown before the local priest, who, before he died,
Humbly begged forgiveness, and of a girl trapped
Hours with her mother, who, in that close darkness,
Learned the riddle of her birth. At last, near dawn,
The spades and picks were set aside, and, once more,
The congregation gathered by the ruined church,
There to make an offering and recite their prayer,
And to remind themselves, again, of what the Jews
Had known: "That Heaven strikes with greatest sorrow
Whom It loves the most." And then, as benediction,
And with that piety one feels close to others' deaths,
There came the lighting of the candles, a modest rite
That in the midst of all those dead and given up,
And the waste that lay across the nearby slopes,
Grew to seem a strange, discreet, and human act.

Robley Wilson, Jr.

Moving Out

Comfort is nothing, you say,
believing you have forgot
all of that: Love, clocks,
butter, and the train to work;
the quarrels of the children
insisting Wake up, Wake up,
the warm bed, the carpets.

How natural to know peace.
You say that; you believe it
for a week—but the slow owls
no matter how they ponder
can think only of mice,
and in the short afternoons
branches break of themselves.

If you have brought a rifle
you take aim at the white sun;
if a rope, you set your snares
wherever the tracks appear;
if an axe, you sharpen it,
you mark the trunks of pines,
you call the thick pitch blood.

James Wright

To the Cicada

(Anacreon)

A few minutes ago
I got up out of the burlap rags somebody
Flung last night into the corner
Of the stone floor.

I am standing here in the field.
I have got my back turned on the whitewashed wall of the house.
The sunlight glances off it and flays
The back of my neck.

It's not yet noon,
But noon is gathering and solidifying,
Splotching my shoulders.
My eyelids weigh ten pounds. Nevertheless,
I lift them open with my fingers.
It's hard to bend the joints.

But there it is,
On the other side of the field,
The water barrel, the only real thing
Left in the shadow.
I can see the rust-stained bung dribbling
Its cold slaver down the curved slats,
Squiggling into black muck beneath
The barbed-wire fence.

Here, now,
Sick of the dry dirt, the southern barrenness,
The Ohio hillside twenty-five miles lost
Away from the river,
I feel my shoulders grow heavier and heavier,
And the dead corn-blades coiling,
Stinging my thighs.
Here,

Just as in the airless corner
Of the barn over the hill
The disinfected hooks stand arranged
Along one wall at head height,
Where the farmer has screwed them in;
Just there where he'd hung them after he'd finished
Dusting out the doorway, hopelessly scattering
Stray wheatbeards, tiny dry blossoms of hay,
Mouse-droppings, cow-pies jagged and cruel
As old gravestones knocked down and scarred faceless;
And just as the meathooks, gleaming softly, hold
Long sidemeat crusted with salt and the dull hams
Gone rigid with smoke,
And the hooks creak as the meat sags, just so
My bones sag and hold up
The flesh of my body.

Still, now, I hear you, singing,
A lightness beginning among the dark crevices,
In the underbark of the locust, beyond me,
The other edge of the field.
A lightness,
You begin tuning up for your time,
Twilight, that belongs to you, deeper and cooler beyond
The barbed wire of this field, even beyond
The Ohio River twenty-five miles away,
Where the Holy Rollers rage all afternoon
And all evening among the mud cracks,
The polluted shore, their voices splintering
Like beetles' wings in a hobo jungle fire,
Their voices heavy as blast furnace fumes, their brutal
Jesus risen but dumb.

But you, lightness,
Light flesh singing lightly,
Trembling in perfect balance on the underbark,
The locust tree of the southeast, you, friendly
To whatever sings in me as it climbs and holds on
Among the damp brambles:

You, lightness,
How were you born in this place, this heavy stone
Plummeting into the stars?
And still you are here. One morning
I found you asleep on a locust root, and carefully
I breathed on your silver body speckled with brown
And held you a while in my palm
And let you sleep.
You, lightness, kindlier than my human body,
Yet somehow friendly to the music in my body,
I let you sleep, one of the gods who will rise
Without being screamed at.

Honey

My father died at the age of eighty. One of the last things he did in his life was to call his fifty-eight-year-old son-in-law "honey." One afternoon in the early 1930's, when I bloodied my head by pitching over a wall at the bottom of a hill and believed that the mere sight of my own blood was the tragic meaning of life, I heard my father offer to murder his future son-in-law. His son-in-law is my brother-in-law, whose name is Paul. These two grown men rose above me and knew that a human life is murder. They weren't fighting about Paul's love for my sister. They were fighting with each other because one strong man, a factory worker, was laid off from his work, and the other strong man, the driver of a coal-truck, was laid off from his work. They were both determined to live their lives, and so they glared at each other and said they were going to live, come hell or high water. High water is not trite in southern Ohio. Nothing is trite along a river. My father died a good death. To die a good death means to live one's life. I don't say a good life.
     I say a life.

Paul Zimmer

Zimmer to His Students

Almost as much as my sins,
I detest poems about poetry;
But, my dear friends, we must
Do things to save ourselves!
Thousands of us, at this moment,
Are fearing death by disregard.
Let me counsel you:

Pay attention to that which you take
For granted. Poetry comes to you
Like puberty, fervent, perplexing,
Unexpected, before you know what
Is happening. It is a humbling process,
Leading to knowledge that can preserve you.

Sometimes when you lie on your back
In an open field and gaze
Up at the sky, you imagine
It is a blank piece of paper.
Your terror rises and you fear
You will plunge out into the vast,
Blue void forever. Then you will
Find that your body yearns
To sink roots, that you can
Save yourself only by clutching
To the constant tufts of grass.

Contributors

DANNIE ABSE was born and educated in Cardiff, South Wales, and now practices medicine in London. Author of eight poetry collections and three prose books, Abse has been president of the British Poetry Society since 1979 and is a Fellow of the Royal Society of Literature. His books most easily available in America include *Collected Poems 1948–1976* and *One-Legged On Ice* (1983).

BETTY ADCOCK's two books are *Walking Out* (1975) and *Nettles* (1983). After ten years in the advertising business, she shifted to teaching at Meredith College in Raleigh, North Carolina, where she is Kenan Writer-in-Residence.

CONRAD AIKEN (1889–1973) authored more than twenty-five books, from *Earth Triumphant and Other Tales in Verse* (1914) through *The Clerk's Journal* (1971). He lived his first eleven and last eleven years in Savannah, and during his career he was honored with nearly every poetry award available to Americans. His poem reprinted here, "The Walk," is one he wrote in 1950 while serving as Consultant in Poetry at the Library of Congress; he was at that time absorbed in writing his autobiography *Ushant*, the complex structure of which is built upon a dream walk.

HEATHER ALLEN lives in New York City, where she is at work on a book of poems and on studies of Georges Braque, Paul Klee, and Vladimir Nabokov.

JOHN ASHBERY's numerous collections include *Some Trees* (1956), *A Wave* (1984), and *Selected Poems* (1985). Born in Rochester, New York, and for many years now a resident of New York City, Ashbery is a highly regarded art critic as well as a poet whom Harold Bloom has called the greatest of the late twentieth century. His *Self-Portrait in a Convex Mirror* (1975) won the Pulitzer Prize, the National Book Award, and the National Book Critics Circle Award; in 1985 he shared the Bollingen Prize in Poetry with Fred Chappell.

COLEMAN BARKS has published three collections of his own poems (*The Juice, New Words*, and *We're Laughing at the Damage*) and three translations of the Sufi master Rumi. Barks is an associate professor of English at the University of Georgia.

GERALD W. BARRAX, born in Attalla, Alabama, moved to Pittsburgh where he eventually attended Duquesne and the University of Pittsburgh. He currently teaches at North Carolina State University, where he edits *Obsidian II: Black Literature in Review*. His poems have appeared in many journals and in three volumes: *Another Kind of Rain*, *An Audience of One*, and *The Deaths of Animals and Lesser Gods*.

ROBIN BEHN's poems have appeared in many journals, including *Field* and *Ironwood*, and she has completed her first book manuscript. She teaches writing, literature, and women's studies at Knox College in Illinois.

ROBERT BLY is a leading theorist of poetry as well as a practicing poet. His earliest collections of poems were *Silence in the Snowy Fields* (1962) and *The Light Around the Body* (1967), while his latest include *Loving a Woman in Two Worlds* and *Selected Poems* (1986). Among his books of essays are *Leaping Poetry*; *News of the Universe: Poems of Two-Fold Consciousness*; and *A Little Book on the Human Shadow*.

[211]

PHILIP BOOTH's *Relations* (1986) contains both new poems and selections from his six books released between 1950 and 1985. Born in New Hampshire, he lives part of the year in a fifth-generation family home in Castine, Maine, and spends the balance teaching writing at Syracuse University.

ANDREA HOLLANDER BUDY was born in Berlin but was reared and educated in the United States; she now resides in Mountain View, Arkansas. She holds an advanced degree in the interpretation of oral literatures, has written and directed drama, and has published a poetry chapbook, *Living on the Cusp* (1981).

KATHRYN STRIPLING BYER's first published poem appeared in *The Georgia Review* in 1969. In 1978 she won the Anne Sexton Poetry Award, judged that year by Maxine Kumin. Her book, *The Girl in the Midst of the Harvest*, came out in 1985 as a winner in the Associated Writing Programs Award Series. A native of southwest Georgia, she lives now in Cullowhee, North Carolina.

MICHAEL CADNUM has one collection of poems published (*The Morning of the Massacre*) and two others forthcoming (*Long Afternoons* and *Amelia*). He has also written several novels and has had short stories in *Kansas Quarterly* and other periodicals. Cadnum lives in a very foggy town across the Bay from San Francisco.

FRED CHAPPELL, who also appeared in our fiction retrospective, teaches English at the University of North Carolina at Greensboro. His major poetic achievement thus far has been the tetralogy *Midquest*, which led to his being named co-winner (with John Ashbery) of the 1985 Bollingen Prize in Poetry. *The Fred Chappell Reader*, containing selections from his many volumes of poetry and fiction, will be out in 1987.

KELLY CHERRY's large output of work includes four novels, two poetry chapbooks, and two full-length books of poems (*Lovers and Agnostics* and *Relativity: A Point of View*). Currently a professor of English at the University of Wisconsin at Madison, she is at work on a nonfiction account of her experiences with psychiatry and psychotherapists.

KEVIN CLARK edited *California Quarterly* (1980–82) while doing graduate work in literature and creative writing at the University of California at Davis. He has published a poetry chapbook, *Granting the Wolf*, and he is writing a critical study of the contemporary long poem in America.

PETER COOLEY, originally from the Midwest, is now teaching at Tulane University in New Orleans. His books include *The Company of Strangers*, *Nightseasons*, and *The Van Gogh Notebooks* (forthcoming in the fall of 1987). He is poetry editor for *The North American Review*.

STEPHEN COREY was an assistant professor of English at the University of South Carolina and the editor of *The Devil's Millhopper* when "Bread" first appeared in *The Georgia Review*. He has published four collections of poems, among them *The Last Magician* (1981) and *Synchronized Swimming* (1985).

CARL DENNIS was born in St. Louis and lives now in Buffalo, where he teaches at the State University of New York. His books are *A House of My Own* (1974), *Climbing Down* (1976), *Signs and Wonders* (1979), and *The Near World* (1985).

WILLIAM DICKEY's first book, *Of the Festivity*, was selected by W. H. Auden as the winner in the Yale Younger Poets Series in 1959. His more recent books include

Brief Lives and *The King of the Golden River*. Born and reared in the Pacific Northwest, Dickey has taught at San Francisco State University since 1962.

WAYNE DODD, a founding editor of *The Ohio Review*, is the author of books for children and young adults, in addition to having published four collections of poems. His newest poetry volume is *Sometimes Music Rises* (1986). A professor of English at Ohio University, Dodd has held both NEA and Ohio Arts Council Fellowships.

WILLIAM DORESKI, who writes criticism as well as poetry, teaches at Keene State College in New Hampshire. Subjects of his recently published essays are Robert Lowell and Emily Dickinson, while his books include *Half of the Map* (1980) and *Earth That Sings: The Poetry of Andrew Glaze* (1985).

RITA DOVE's three full-length books of poetry include *Museum* (1983) and *Thomas and Beulah* (1986); her short fiction collection, *Fifth Sunday* (1985), was the inaugural volume in the Callaloo Fiction Series. Currently the poetry editor for *Callaloo*, she teaches at Arizona State University.

STEPHEN DUNN received the Distinguished Poetry Fellowship from the New Jersey Arts Council in 1986. He is the author of six published books, the most recent being *Local Time* (1986), a winner of the National Poetry Series open competition. Dunn teaches at Stockton State College (New Jersey) and at Columbia University.

CHARLES EDWARD EATON, whose poems have appeared in *The Georgia Review* during every decade of its existence, studied under Robert Frost at Harvard. In addition to producing nine volumes of poems and three of short stories, he has written extensively on American painting and was for four years the American Vice-Consul in Rio de Janeiro. His newest book is *The Work of the Wrench* (1985).

GARY EDDY, whose Ph.D. from the State University of New York at Binghamton is in modern poetry and rhetoric, has published criticism and poems in many magazines. He lives near Flagstaff, Arizona, where he is completing *That*, a poetry collection.

LYNN EMANUEL's *Hotel Fiesta* received the Great Lakes College Association Award in 1985; it was also one of sixty books selected by the NEA to represent the United States at the International Feminist Book Fair in Oslo, Norway, during the summer of 1986. Emanuel teaches at the University of Pittsburgh.

JOHN ENGELS teaches English at St. Michael's College in Vermont. The latest of his five volumes of poems is *Weather-Fear: New and Selected Poems, 1958–1982* (University of Georgia Press).

MARK A. R. FACKNITZ is currently living in Vanves, France, where he is writing a novel. He has published poems, fiction, and criticism in *The Louisville Review*, *Iowa Review*, *Studies in Short Fiction*, and elsewhere.

ALICE FRIMAN has authored two chapbooks, *A Question of Innocence* and *Song to My Sister*, and edited *Loaves and Fishes: A Book of Indiana Women Poets*. She teaches at the University of Indianapolis.

ROBERT FROST (1874–1963) is perhaps the one poet of our century who literally needs no introduction. The complete body of his work—eleven volumes, from

A Boy's Will (1913) through *In the Clearing* (1962)—remains available in virtually every bookstore and library in the United States. "From a Milkweed Pod" was privately printed as Frost's "Christmas Poem" for 1954 prior to its appearance in *The Georgia Review* in the fall of the next year; then, under the title "Pod of the Milkweed," it was reprinted in his final collection.

ALICE FULTON's first book, *Dance Script with Electric Ballerina* (the title poem of which appears in this retrospective), won the AWP Poetry Award in 1982; her second, *Palladium*, was a winner in the National Poetry Series of 1985. Widely published also as an essayist and reviewer, she teaches at the University of Michigan.

BRENDAN GALVIN's three most recent books—*Seals in the Inner Harbor* (1986), *Winter Oysters* (1983), and *Atlantic Flyway* (1980)—have titles reflective of the fact that he holds a degree in natural sciences as well as two in literature and writing. Since 1969 he has taught at Connecticut State University.

JAMES GALVIN lives part-time in Iowa City and part-time in Tie Siding, Wyoming. His books of poetry are *Imaginary Timber* and *God's Mistress*.

DAN GERBER has published several poetry collections, a nonfiction book on the Indianapolis 500, novels, and stories in such magazines as *The New Yorker* and *Playboy*. He lives in Michigan.

GARY GILDNER's new and selected poems, *Blue Like the Heavens* (1984), was his eighth collection. A Michigan native who has lived in France, Mexico, the Pacific Northwest, and the Midwest, he has written much fiction in recent years: one collection of stories (*The Crush*) came out in 1983; another is scheduled for 1987, when his first novel (*The Second Bridge*) will also be released.

DAVID GRAHAM, whose first book is *Magic Shows* (Cleveland State University Poetry Center), teaches at North Carolina State University. His poems have appeared in *Poetry*, *Nimrod*, and elsewhere.

JORIE GRAHAM's second book, *Erosions*, was nominated for the National Book Critics Circle Award; her third, *The End of Beauty*, will be published soon. A faculty member of the Iowa Writers' Workshop, she is also a reviewer for *The New York Times Book Review*.

ROBERT GRAVES (1895–1985) built a canon of writings the scope of which is perhaps unsurpassed in our century. *A Survey of Modernist Poetry* (1927), coauthored with Laura Riding, remains an insightful and crucial commentary on the poetry of our own time; *Goodbye to All That* (1929), his early autobiography, is one of the finest commentaries on the World War I era in England; his two 1934 novels, *I, Claudius* and *Claudius the God*, present controversial rewrites of history; and *The White Goddess: A Historical Grammar of Poetic Myth* (1947) provides one of the century's most comprehensive and idiosyncratic poetics. All of this work, and more, was in addition to the many volumes of lyric poetry Graves produced before failing health drove him into near silence during the last decade of his life.

DEBORA GREGER has lived in England for several years at different times, once on an Amy Lowell Traveling Poetry Scholarship. Author of *Movable Islands* and *And*, she teaches creative writing at the University of Florida.

JEANINE HATHAWAY has been teaching in the MFA program at Wichita State University since 1974. Her poem "Magnificat" recently won *Kansas Quarterly*'s Seaton Award, and she is now completing a novel based on her years as a Catholic nun.

HUNT HAWKINS, who writes poems at a rate of three or four per year, is widely published as a Conrad scholar. He hopes to have enough poems to put together a book before the decade is over; meanwhile, he teaches and writes at Florida State University.

ANTHONY HECHT's many honors include the Pulitzer Prize, the Bollingen Prize, and the Eugenio Montale Award. His books of poetry include *A Summoning of Stones, The Hard Hours, Millions of Strange Shadows*, and *The Venetian Vespers*, while his most recent publication is *Obbligati: Essays in Criticism*. He is University Professor in the graduate school of Georgetown University.

WILLIAM HEYEN has published a dozen books and anthologies of poetry and criticism, among them *The Swastika Poems; Erika: Poems of the Holocaust; A Profile of Theodore Roethke;* and *The Generation of 2000: Contemporary American Poets*. A visiting teacher at many schools, he has been based at SUNY-Brockport since 1967.

JONATHAN HOLDEN's most recent publications are *The Names of the Rapids* (winner of the 1985 Juniper Prize), and a book of criticism, *Style and Authenticity in Postmodern Poetry*.

JOHN HOLLANDER, professor of English at Yale University, has collaborated on solo, choral, and operatic works in addition to producing his own poetry and criticism. His volumes of poems include *Powers of Thirteen* (1983) and *In Time and Place* (1986); among his critical works are *The Figure of Echo* and *Rhyme's Reason*, both released in 1981.

RICHARD HOWARD is one of our premier translators of French literature as well as a Pulitzer Prize-winning poet and a widely recognized critic. His ninth poetry collection, *No Traveller*, is due out in 1987. His version of Baudelaire's *Les Fleurs du Mal* won the American Book Award for Translation in 1983, the same year that he earned the *PEN* medal for translation. He lives in New York City.

RICHARD HUGO (1923–1982) published nine books of poems and a collection of essays (*The Triggering Town*) between 1961 and 1981. *Making Certain It Goes On* brought together all of his poems in a 1984 posthumous collection; a similar gathering of his many essays, *The Real West Marginal Way: A Poet's Autobiography*, was published in 1986. A Boeing Aircraft employee who eventually became director of the creative-writing program at the University of Montana, Hugo earned a wide audience and many awards in the last years of his life.

T. R. HUMMER teaches at Kenyon College. In 1987 the University of Illinois Press will bring out his fourth book of poems: *Lower-Class Heresy*.

RICHARD JACKSON edits *The Poetry Miscellany* and is the author of two books of poetry, *Part of the Story* and *Worlds Apart*. He has also published *Acts of Mind: Conversations with Contemporary Poets* and *Dismantling Time in Contemporary Poetry*.

PAMELA KIRCHER, whose poem in this volume was her first publication, has placed her work subsequently in *The Ohio Review, Tendril, raccoon*, and elsewhere. She is a librarian at Ohio University.

JUDITH KITCHEN's *Perennials* (the title poem of which is reprinted here) was published in 1985 as the winner of the Anhinga Prize. In addition to her poetry, she has

[215]

authored short stories and reviews, while serving as editor/publisher of State Street Press.

WILLIAM KLOEFKORN works with the Nebraska Poets-in-the-Schools program and teaches at Nebraska Wesleyan College. Among his books are *Honeymoon* and *A Life Like Mine*. In 1978 he won the Nebraska hog-calling championship.

TED KOOSER lives in Lincoln, Nebraska, where he is an executive for a life insurance company. His latest book is *Blizzard Voices* (Bieler Press).

MAXINE KUMIN won the Pulitzer Prize in 1973 for *Up Country*; her eighth book, *The Long Approach*, was issued in 1985. A former Consultant in Poetry to the Library of Congress (1981–1982) and occasionally a visiting faculty member at Princeton, Brandeis, and other universities, Kumin raises horses on her New Hampshire farm.

GREG KUZMA has edited *Pebble* magazine for nearly twenty years and is preparing a special anniversary issue. He also runs the Best Cellar Press, for which he recently edited the anthology *Poems for the Dead*. The latest of his own collections is *Of China and Of Greece* (1984).

SYDNEY LEA's books are *Searching the Drowned Man* (1980), *The Floating Candles* (1982), and—scheduled for 1987 release—*No Sign*. Founder of the *New England Review*, he teaches at Middlebury College.

PHILIP LEVINE's *Selected Poems* (1984) highlights his first ten books, from *On the Edge* (1963) through *The Names of the Lost* (1976) and *One for the Rose* (1981). Born and reared in Detroit, he has lived in Iowa, Spain, and California. After many years of teaching at Fresno State University, he has recently taken a position at Tufts University.

SUSAN LUDVIGSON will soon publish her third Louisiana State University Press collection, *The Beautiful Noon of No Shadow*. A member of the English faculty at Winthrop College in Rock Hill, South Carolina, she has used Guggenheim, Fulbright, and NEA grants to spend most of the past few years living in Europe.

DEXTER MASTERS, formerly the director of Consumers Union and editor of *Consumer Reports*, has resided for many years now in Devon, England. In addition to poetry he has published two novels: *The Accident* (1955) and *The Cloud Chamber* (1971).

SUMIO MATSUDA has taught English at East Los Angeles College for the past twenty years. His poems have appeared in *Epos*, *Ann Arbor Review*, *Bitteroot*, and elsewhere.

JACK MATTHEWS, also featured in our fiction retrospective, has written mostly novels and short fiction. One of his collections of stories, *Dubious Persuasions*, has just been published in a Spanish translation in Argentina. Soon to be released is *Booking in the Heartland*, a volume of essays on rare books and book collecting.

WILLIAM MATTHEWS taught at the University of Washington and elsewhere before settling in New York City recently. His books include *Running the New Road* (1970), *Flood* (1982), *A Happy Childhood* (1984), and *Foreseeable Futures* (forthcoming in 1987).

MEKEEL MCBRIDE's most recent book is *The Going Under of the Evening Land* (1983). An associate professor of English at the University of New Hampshire, she has taught previously at Wheaton, Harvard, and Princeton.

MARTHA MCFERREN has recently entered the MFA writing program at Warren Wilson College. Author of two collections (*Delusions of a Popular Mind* and *Get Me Out of Here!*) with a third forthcoming, she lives in New Orleans, where she is active in local and regional poetry programs.

PETER MEINKE, after several collections of poems over the past ten years, has been writing more and more fiction. His first book of stories, *The Piano Tuner* (1986), won the Flannery O'Connor Award from the University of Georgia Press. He is director of the writing program at Eckerd College.

JAMES MERRILL's career was highlighted in 1982 by the appearance of both his selected poems (*From the First Nine: Poems 1946–1976*) and *The Changing Light at Sandover*, his epic, multivolume work that includes *Divine Comedies*; *Mirabell: Books of Number*; and *Scripts for the Pageant*. His newest efforts are *Late Settings* (poems) and *The Image Maker*, a one-act play that debuted in Los Angeles in early 1986.

W. S. MERWIN's education as a poet and translator included serving as tutor of Robert Graves's children on Majorca. The first of Merwin's nearly thirty books was *A Mask for Janus* (1952); his most recent include *Four French Plays*, *From the Spanish Morning*, and *Opening the Hand*.

JANE MILLER, a 1985 recipient of a NEA fellowship, has just finished a new collection of poems to be entitled *American Odalisque*. She recently published a collaborative volume, *Black Holes, Black Stockings*, with Olga Broumas.

SCOTT MINAR is a lifelong resident of Ohio. In addition to writing, he is pursuing a career as a professional musician with his band, The Kings of Hollywood. When "Luminare" appeared in *The Georgia Review* in 1984 it marked Minar's first publication in a national journal.

JUDSON MITCHAM has had poems in many magazines over the past few years; his first collection, *Notes for a Prayer in June*, is in the State Street Press chapbook series. Mitcham teaches psychology at Fort Valley State College in Georgia.

MARION MONTGOMERY has published fourteen books, including three collections of poems and three novels. Several years ago he completed a trilogy of critical books on American literature, *The Prophetic Poet and the Spirit of the Age*. Professor of English at the University of Georgia for more than thirty years, he is retiring in 1987 to write and lecture full time.

W. R. MOSES notes that since adolescence he has been "really more concerned with writing poetry than with any other activity, yet never prolific. Always more or less out of tune with my times—a fact which I do not regret." Professor emeritus at Kansas State University, Moses counts among his books *Identities* (1965), *Passage* (1976), and *Double View* (1984). In 1940 he had a section in the New Directions volume *Five Young American Poets*, which also included John Berryman and Randall Jarrell.

MICHAEL MOTT, in addition to his four books of poems, has published an award-winning biography, *The Seven Mountains of Thomas Merton*, and novels for both adults and children. Born in London, he has lived and taught in America since 1966; he is currently at Bowling Green State University in Ohio.

LISEL MUELLER's *The Private Life* was the Lamont Poetry Selection for 1975, while *The Need to Hold Still* won the American Book Award for 1981. Her newest volume of poems is *Second Language* (1986). She has also done several books of translations from German (her native tongue); *New Letters* (Summer 1986) printed her prose memoir about returning to visit Germany after a forty-four year absence.

HOWARD NEMEROV's more than twenty books include poetry, essays, novels, and short fiction. *The Collected Poems of Howard Nemerov* won both the Pulitzer Prize and the National Book Award in 1978, with many other honors preceding and following these. He has been associated with Washington University in St. Louis since 1969.

JOHN FREDERICK NIMS—poet, translator, and editor—holds a Ph.D in comparative literature from the University of Chicago. The most recent of his six books are *The Kiss: A Jambalaya* and *Selected Poems*, both published in 1982. His volumes of translations are *The Poems of St. John of the Cross* and *Sappho to Valery*. From 1978–1984 he was the editor of *Poetry*, and he has authored one of the most popular introductory poetry texts, *Western Wind*.

JOYCE CAROL OATES finds time to help Raymond Smith edit *The Ontario Review* even though she works steadily on novels, poetry, and short fiction. ("The Ballerina" appeared in our fiction retrospective.) A professor of English at Princeton University, she is a past winner of the National Book Award and is a member of the American Academy–Institute of Arts and Letters.

MARY OLIVER, winner of the Pulitzer Prize in 1984 for *American Primitive*, lives in Massachusetts and occasionally teaches; she has been poet-in-residence at Bucknell University and the University of Cincinnati. Her other books include *No Voyage* (1965), *Twelve Moons* (1979), and *Dream Work* (1986).

ROBERT PACK teaches at Middlebury College and has directed the Bread Loaf Writers' Conference since 1972. *Waking to My Name* (1980) brought together a new collection plus selections from his first five books; it has been followed by *Faces in a Single Tree* (1984) and *Affirming Limits* (1985), while *Clayfeld Rejoices, Clayfeld Laments* is forthcoming.

LINDA PASTAN lives in Potomac, Maryland. Her six books include *Aspects of Eve* (1975), *PM/AM: New and Selected Poems* (1983—nominated for the American Book Award), and *A Fraction of Darkness* (1985).

ALICE GOLEMBIEWSKI PHILLIPS had her first national publication in *The Georgia Review* (Summer 1978). Her chapbook *The Bone Orchard* appeared in the 1980 Inland Boat series. After several years at *The New Yorker* and *The Village Voice*, she is now working for the *TLS* in London.

STANLEY PLUMLY is currently at the University of Maryland. Among his books are *In the Outer Dark* (winner of the Delmore Schwartz Memorial Award), *Out-of-the-Body Travel*, and *Summer Celestial*. Born and reared in the Ohio Valley, he was one of the founding editors of *The Ohio Review* and has taught at the Universities of Washington, Houston, and Iowa.

Bin Ramke's *The Difference Between Night and Day* was chosen by Richard Hugo for the Yale Younger Poets Series in 1977. His subsequent books are *White Monkeys* (1981) and *The Language Student* (1986). Ramke teaches at the University of Denver, where he directs the writing program and is poetry editor for *The Denver Quarterly*.

Byron Herbert Reece (1917–1958) was born and reared in the secluded mountains of North Georgia. As a child he read *The Pilgrim's Progress* and most of the Bible before starting elementary school; as an adult he was a mostly hermit-like farmer. Winner of two Guggenheim fellowships, he published a novel (*Better a Dinner of Herbs*) and five collections of poetry (*Ballad of the Bones, Bow Down in Jericho, The Season of Flesh, The Hawk and the Sun,* and *A Song of Joy*). He committed suicide in 1958 in Young Harris, Georgia.

David Rigsbee has translated the Russian of Mikhail Lermontov and Joseph Brodsky, edited *The Ardis Anthology of New American Poetry* (1977), and published two volumes of his own work: *Stamping Ground* and *The Hopper Light* (both in 1986). He lives in Baton Rouge and on the island of Jamaica.

Pattiann Rogers, who now lives in Texas, completed her studies at the University of Houston. Her books are *The Expectations of Light* (1981) and *The Tattooed Lady in the Garden* (1986). A frequent contributor to *Poetry Northwest*, she has won that magazine's Theodore Roethke Prize as well as grants from the Guggenheim Foundation and the NEA.

Jay Rogoff was born in New York City and educated at the University of Pennsylvania and Syracuse University. He now lives near Saratoga Springs and teaches in Skidmore College's prison program. His long poetic sequence, "First Hand," won the 1982 John Masefield Memorial Award from the Poetry Society of America and will be issued as a chapbook by Tamarack Press.

Reg Saner's books are *Climbing into the Roots* (winner of the 1975 Walt Whitman Award), *So This Is the Map* (winner of the 1981 National Poetry Series open competition), and *Essay on Air* (1984). He teaches at the University of Colorado in Boulder.

Penelope Scambly Schott has recently published a novel, *A Little Ignorance* (1986), and a poetry chapbook, *My Grandparents Were Married for Sixty-Five Years*. She lives on the Delaware and Raritan Canal in New Jersey.

Philip Schultz founded and directs a private school, the Writers' Studio, in New York City. His collection *Like Wings* won the American Academy–Institute of Arts and Letters Award in 1979, and *Deep within the Ravine* earned the Lamont Prize in 1984.

Bettie M. Sellers, recently named Goolsby Professor of English at Young Harris College, is the author of five poetry collections, including *Liza's Monday* (1986). Born in Florida, she has spent most of her life in North Georgia.

Anne Sexton (1928–1974) is, along with Robert Lowell, Sylvia Plath, and W. D. Snodgrass, among those poets most often associated with the "confessional school" of writing. (She studied under Lowell and has noted her debt to Snodgrass' 1959 book, *Heart's Needle*.) Among her own books are *To Bedlam and Part Way Back* (1960), *Live or Die* (1966), *Transformations* (1971), and *The Book of Folly*

(1973). She killed herself in October 1974, two months before the poems reprinted here were originally published in *The Georgia Review*.

CHARLES SIMIC was born in Yugoslavia and lived there for a decade before emigrating to the United States. His *Selected Poems 1963–1983* brings together work from such volumes as *Dismantling the Silence*, *Return to a Place Lit by a Glass of Milk*, and *Charon's Cosmology*; his latest collection is *Unending Blues*. Simic teaches at the University of New Hampshire.

CATHY SMITH-BOWERS' poems have appeared in *Southern Poetry Review*, *Cincinnati Review*, and other places. Winner of a fellowship in 1984 to Exeter College, Oxford, she teaches at Queens College in Charlotte, North Carolina.

DAVE SMITH, a prolific poet and essayist (with a novel also to his credit), published two new volumes in 1986, *The Roundhouse Voices: Selected and New Poems* and *Local Assays: On Contemporary American Poetry*. Professor of English and Distinguished Scholar at Virginia Commonwealth University in his native state, he has taught in the past at the University of Utah, the University of Florida, and elsewhere.

JORDAN SMITH's books are *An Apology for Loving the Old Hymns* (1982) and *Lucky Seven* (scheduled for 1987). He lives in Burnt Hills, New York, and teaches at Union College.

ELIZABETH SPIRES is the author of *Globe* (1981) and *Swan's Land* (1985). She is now on an Amy Lowell Traveling Poetry Scholarship in London, where she is working on a new collection.

CARL L. STACH has had poems in numerous magazines and in a chapbook, *The Animation of Dusk*. He teaches at Illinois Benedictine College and is completing a doctorate through the Harvard Graduate School of Education.

WILLIAM STAFFORD, retired from teaching but still traveling to read and lecture, lives in Lake Oswego, Oregon. He is the author of many volumes, including *Stories That Could Be True: New and Collected Poems* (1977); *A Glass Face in the Rain* (1982); *Segues*, a correspondence in poetry with Marvin Bell (1983), and *An Oregon Message* (1986). Two collections of his prose have appeared in the University of Michigan Press's Poets on Poetry series: *Writing the Australian Crawl* (1978) and *You Must Revise Your Life* (1986).

GERALD STERN's selected poems will be published in 1988 by Harper & Row. His books to date include *Rejoicings*, *Lucky Life*, *The Red Coal*, and *Paradise Poems*. He writes a regular column for *The American Poetry Review* under the title "Notes from the River," and he teaches at the University of Iowa Writers' Workshop.

ALEX STEVENS, who has published in *Poetry*, *The New Yorker*, and elsewhere, has completed his first book manuscript. A former teacher, he currently runs a small publishing business in Houston.

MARK STRAND reports that he has no memory of having written the poem reprinted here. His latest works as poet and translator include *Rembrandt Takes a Walk* and *Travelling in the Family: Selected Poems of Carlos Drummond de Andrade*.

LUCIEN STRYK's *Collected Poems 1953–1983* was published in 1984. He has written a book of essays, *Encounter with Zen*, and he has translated Japanese poetry in several volumes, including *On Love and Barley: Haiku of Basho*; *Triumph of the*

Sparrow: Zen Poems of Shinkichi Takahashi; and *The Penguin Book of Zen Poetry*. Stryk presently holds a research professorship at Northern Illinois University.

DYAN SUBLETT will be on sabbatical in 1987 to complete work on a collection of poems; she is Director of Development at Hampshire College in Amherst, Massachusetts. *Poetry, The Ohio Review*, and other magazines have featured her work.

MARY SWANDER won a "Discovery"/*The Nation* Award in 1976 and published her first book, *Succession*, in 1979. She has since published two more collections, *Driving the Body Back* and *Lost Lake* (both in 1986), and has held two fellowships from the Ingram Merrill Foundation.

DAVID SWANGER teaches aesthetic education and creative writing at the University of California at Santa Cruz. His professional articles have appeared in *The Journal of Aesthetic Education, Educational Theory*, and elsewhere. Ithaca House has published his two books of poems, *The Shape of Waters* and *Inside the Horse*.

DENNIS TRUDELL has six chapbooks, the newest being *Imagining a Revolution: Poems about Central America*. A teacher at the University of Wisconsin in Whitewater, he has also written two novels (unpublished) for young adults.

CHARLES VANDERSEE, a Henry Adams scholar at the University of Virginia, wrote "Spring at Arm's Length" (in this collection) while in Boston editing *The Letters of Henry Adams* for Harvard University Press. His poems have appeared in magazines and in such unlikely anthologies as *American Classic: Car Poems for Collectors*.

ELLEN BRYANT VOIGT has taught at Goddard College and Massachusetts Institute of Technology; she is now on the staff of the MFA Writing Program at Warren Wilson College. Her books are *Claiming Kin* (1976) and *The Forces of Plenty* (1983).

DAVID WAGONER has published fourteen books of poems, most recently *First Light* (1983), and ten novels. Since 1954 he has been on the faculty of the University of Washington, where, since 1966, he has edited *Poetry Northwest*. His work also appeared in *The Georgia Review*'s fiction retrospective.

MARILYN NELSON WANIEK, whose first published poem appeared in *The Georgia Review* (Spring 1978), teaches at the University of Connecticut in Storrs. She has published *For the Body* (1978) and *Mama's Promises* (1985), and she has written verse for children. The NEA, the Danforth Foundation, and the Cultural Ministry of Denmark have awarded her fellowships.

ROBERT PENN WARREN was recently named as the first Poet Laureate of the United States—the latest recognition of his standing as America's leading man of letters. Of his more than fifty published titles (excluding the numerous volumes he has edited or coedited) the most recent include *Chief Joseph of the Nez Perce*, 1983 (first published in its entirety in the Summer 1982 issue of *The Georgia Review*), and *New and Selected Poems: 1923–1985*.

ROSANNA WARREN is an essayist, reviewer, and translator as well as a poet. *Each Leaf Shines Separate* (poems) appeared in 1985; forthcoming works include a biography of Max Jacob and a translation (with Stephen Scully) of Euripides' *The Suppliant Women*.

MICHAEL WATERS has traveled widely in recent years, living for extended periods in Greece, Costa Rica, and Thailand. Based now at Salisbury State College in Maryland, he has also taught at Ohio University and the University of Athens, Greece. His books include *Fish Light* (1975), *Not Just Any Death* (1979), and *Anniversary of the Air* (1985).

DAVID WEISS's first two poetry collections were both released in 1986: *The Pail of Steam*, a chapbook, and *The Fourth Part of the World*, a full-length volume published as the winner of the George Elliston Poetry Prize. Weiss teaches at Hobart and William Smith Colleges in upstate New York.

NORMAN WILLIAMS graduated from the Yale University Law School and has a practice in Vermont. He has held fellowships from the Amy Lowell and the Ingram Merrill Foundations; his first book, *The Unlovely Child*, came out in 1985.

ROBLEY WILSON, JR., perhaps best known for his short fiction and for his work as the editor of *The North American Review*, recently won the 1986 Agnes Lynch Starrett Prize and will have his first volume of poems, *Kingdoms of the Ordinary*, published in 1987. His books of stories include *Dancing for Men*, the winner of the 1982 Drue Heinz Literature Prize.

JAMES WRIGHT (1927–1980) was born in Martin's Ferry, Ohio, and died in New York City. His first book, *The Green Wall*, was selected by W. H. Auden as the 1957 winner in the Yale Younger Poets Series. His other books include *The Branch Will Not Break* (1963), *Shall We Gather at the River* (1968), *Two Citizens* (1974), *To a Blossoming Pear Tree* (1977), and the posthumous *This Journey* (1982). Among Wright's many honors were the Pulitzer Prize and the Melville Cane Award, both received in 1972 for his *Collected Poems*.

PAUL ZIMMER, founder of the Pitt Poetry Series and former director of the University of Georgia Press, currently heads the University of Iowa Press. His *Family Reunion: New and Selected Poems* (1983) contains work from *The Zimmer Poems* (1976), *With Wanda: Town and Country Poems* (1980), and other volumes. A suite of his works, "The American Zimmer," was set to music by Robert Russell Bennett and performed by the American Wind Symphony on its bicentennial tour.

Credits

Richard Hugo: "Last Words to James Wright" from *Making Certain It Goes On* (W. W. Norton & Company), © 1984 by The Estate of Richard Hugo. Reprinted by permission of Ripley S. Hugo.

William Matthews: "Flood" (under the title "Flood Time") appears in *Flood: Poems*, ©1981 by William Matthews. Reprinted by permission of Little, Brown and Company in association with the Atlantic Monthly Press.

W. S. Merwin: "Fate" from *The Compass Flower*, © 1977 by W. S. Merwin. Reprinted by permission of Atheneum Publishers, Inc. "Stairs," © 1975 by W. S. Merwin. Reprinted by permission of the author.

W. R. Moses: "Old Theme" from *Identities* (Wesleyan University Press), © 1965 by W. R. Moses.

John Frederick Nims: "Finisterre" from *The Kiss: A Jambalaya*, © 1982 by John Frederick Nims. Reprinted by permission of Houghton Mifflin Company.

Linda Pastan: "The Printer," "Epilogue," and "Prologue" from *PM/AM: New and Selected Poems* (W. W. Norton & Company), © 1982 by Linda Pastan.

Byron Herbert Reece: "Such Instance" from *A Song of Joy*, © 1952 by E. P. Dutton and Company. Reprinted by permission of T. J. Reece.

Pattiann Rogers: "The Creation of the Inaudible" from *The Tattooed Lady in the Garden*, © 1986 by Pattiann Rogers. Reprinted by permission of Wesleyan University Press.

Philip Schultz: "My Guardian Angel Stein" from *Deep within the Ravine*, © 1982 by Philip Schultz. Reprinted by permission of Viking Penguin, Inc.

Anne Sexton: "The Witch's Life," "Locked Doors," and "Snow" from *The Awful Rowing Toward God* by Anne Sexton, © 1975 by Loring Conant, Jr., Executor of the Estate of Anne Sexton. Reprinted by permission of The Sterling Lord Agency, Inc.

Jordan Smith: "For Dulcimer & Doubled Voice" from *An Apology for Loving the Old Hymns*, © 1982 by Princeton University Press. Reprinted by permission of Princeton University Press.

Lucien Stryk: "Savants" from *Collected Poems 1953–1983*, © 1984 by Lucien Stryk. Reprinted by permission of the Ohio University Press.

Ellen Bryant Voigt: "A Fugue" from *The Forces of Plenty*, © 1983 by Ellen Bryant Voigt. Reprinted by permission of the author and the publisher, W. W. Norton and Company, Inc.

Marilyn Nelson Waniek: "It's All in Your Head" from *Mama's Promises* (Louisiana State University Press), © 1985 by Marilyn Nelson Waniek.

Robert Penn Warren: "Muted Music" and "Seasons" from *New and Selected Poems: 1923–1985*, © 1983 by Robert Penn Warren. Reprinted by permission of Random House, Inc.

Rosanna Warren: "Painting a Madonna" from *Each Leaf Shines Separate*, © 1984 by Rosanna Warren. Reprinted by permission of the author and the publisher, W. W. Norton and Company, Inc.

Norman Williams: "The Tremors at Balvano" from *The Unlovely Child*, © 1984 by Norman Williams. Reprinted by permission of Alfred A. Knopf, Inc.

James Wright: "To the Cicada" and "Honey" from *This Journey* by James Wright (Random House), © 1982 by Edith Anne Wright, executrix of the Estate of James Wright. Reprinted by permission of Edith Anne Wright.